Traveling Blind

New Directions in the Human-Animal Bond
Alan M. Beck, series editor

Traveling Blind

Adventures in Vision with a Guide Dog by My Side

Susan Krieger

Purdue University Press
West Lafayette, Indiana

Printed in the United States of America.

Library of Congress Cataloging-in-Publication Data

Krieger, Susan.
  Traveling blind : adventures in vision with a guide dog by my
side / Susan Krieger.
      p. cm. -- (New directions in the human-animal bond)
  Includes bibliographical references.
  ISBN 978-1-55753-557-3
  1. Women with disabilities--Travel--United States. 2. Low
vision--United States. 3. Guide dogs--United States. I. Title.
  HV1569.3.W65K75 2010
  910.4092--dc22
  [B]
                                        2009042877

To obtain an accessible PDF version of this book, please contact
the publisher at pupress@purdue.edu.

Cover photo courtesy of Estelle Freedman.

For Estelle

Contents

Preface

When I began to write *Traveling Blind*, I knew only that I was delighted to be able to see a mountain, its looming figure silhouetted against a stark desert plain. I wanted to write about my trip to that mountain in order to explore issues of blindness. I did not know, at first, that my emerging theme of "traveling blind" would expand to include the adventure of learning to navigate with a guide dog, the pleasures of sharing the road with my intimate partner, my struggles to accept new interdependencies, and my excitement in discovering magnificent vistas, even if I could see them only incompletely.

I wrote this book with my guide dog, Teela, lying at my feet, my computer speaking aloud both her name and mine; I wrote it over a period of several years during which I revisited the desert places I loved, hoping they would not change as quickly as my eyesight. I wanted the book to contribute to broader understandings of blindness, vision, and disability and to encourage readers who might, like me, confront changed circumstances requiring new vision.

Because I have often felt vulnerable and alone when traveling blind, I am deeply grateful to organizations, friends, and colleagues who have given me support. I especially want to thank Guide Dogs for the Blind in San Rafael, California, for the gift of Teela, my golden guide, who leaves her tracks on many of these pages. During my residence at Guide Dogs in 2003, I benefited from the shared life experiences of my classmates and from the generosity and wisdom of the volunteers, staff, and trainers. I am grateful to Teela's "puppy raisers"—Betsy, Galen, Emily, and Spencer McCray—who nurtured and socialized her during her first sixteen months. I thank Jeniece Thomas, Teela's individual trainer on the Guide Dogs campus, who, for the next five months, taught her how to perform guide work so that when I arrived for the last month, she was ready to lead me.

I thank the Program in Feminist Studies and the Clayman Institute for Gender Research at Stanford University for supporting my teaching and research. I am grateful to the students in my courses on Women and Disabilities, who generously shared their insights and were open to mine—particularly to my desire to view disabilities in a positive manner and as a normal part of life, rather than as a circumstance that must set one apart and cause pity or alarm.

While I worked on the manuscript, individuals gave me close readings, encouragement, and editorial advice that was invaluable. I thank especially Paola Gianturco for her warmth and enthusiasm and for caring that all my sentences be clear. Paola, a photojournalist, often helpfully pointed out parallels between my attempts to see with limited sight and her creative efforts with a camera. I thank Lynn Crawford for encouraging my writing and welcoming my alliance with Teela, as well as for her useful editorial suggestions. Susan Christopher, Mary Felstiner, Elaine Tyler May, and Esther Rothblum read the manuscript critically, providing recommendations that improved the whole. Jack Ellis read drafts of the book twice, sending me extensive and affirming comments. Martin Krieger's early and continuing encouragement was crucial. For reading selected chapters and providing supportive feedback, I thank Zandra Contaxis, John D'Emilio, Carmen de Monteflores, Margaret Knight, Ilene Levitt, my mother Rhoda Cahn, and my sister Kathe Morse. For their efforts in moving the book toward publication, I am grateful to Felicia Eth, Pat Holt, Doug Mitchell, and Caroline Pincus.

I thank Alan Beck, who graciously saw possibilities for including *Traveling Blind: Adventures in Vision with a Guide Dog by My Side* in the Purdue University Press series on New Directions in the Human-Animal Bond. The Purdue Press staff—Rebecca Corbin, Katherine Purple, Bryan Shaffer, and Director Charles Watkinson—made the production process move smoothly and insured that the book would be accessible for blind and print-impaired readers.

In *Traveling Blind*, I include many experiences shared with others who appear here under pseudonyms or anonymously and whose generosity and good company has been a gift. I thank especially Phil Norton, Arnold Sargent, Gabby Tamayo, Gerry Tamayo, and Phoebe Wood for exceptional hospitality; Jodi Clark and Natasha Isenhour for experiences at the gallery; and June Hill, L. G. May, the late Ena Osborn, and Cindy Taetz for welcoming two strangers (and a guide dog) who stopped in off the road. I am grateful to Mark Hakela of the Bureau of Land Management, Las Cruces, for initial directions to Big Hatchet, and to the New Mexico Wilderness Alliance for their efforts to preserve special places like "sky islands." I thank the Bear Mountain Lodge in Silver City, run by the Nature Conservancy of New Mexico; the Sierra Grande Lodge and Spa in Truth or Consequences for a uniquely magical night; the ghosts of Hachita old and new; and the town of Socorro for abundant luminarias. During these travels, Zandra Contaxis and Alison Werger watched the home front, caring for our small pet dog Esperanza and our three cats—Katie, Shadow, and Sienna.

Words cannot adequately express my deep feelings of gratitude for Estelle Freedman, whom I call "Hannah" in this book. Estelle both shared in these experiences and improved my writing about them. She has been my editor, my fan club, my home, my delight, my lover, my travel companion, my sighted guide. On our travels, she drove, she watched out for me and Teela, and she often provided me with an extra pair of eyes—describing vividly scenes and details I could not see until I, too, saw them clearly, if only in my mind. These stories are mine but enriched by her love.

Introduction

Traveling Blind is a romance, a travel adventure, an emotional quest, and a book about coming to terms with lack of sight. It explores the invisible work of navigating with a guide dog while learning to perceive the world in new ways. In a previous book, *Things No Longer There: A Memoir of Losing Sight and Finding Vision*, I described my initial experiences of loss of sight. *Traveling Blind* begins where *Things No Longer There* left off. As my eyesight worsened, I began to use a white cane and soon I wanted to have a guide dog. After completing a month-long residential training program, learning to walk with a lively Golden Retriever-Yellow Labrador by my side, I set out on my own, developing confidence as I traveled both local streets and more distant roads and byways. This book is a story of my travels and of lessons learned.

Three months after coming home with my dog, Teela, I began to write *Traveling Blind: Adventures in Vision with a Guide Dog by My Side* to document what felt like a unique experience. Walking with a guide dog, one walks differently, and seeing with partial blindness, one sees differently. As I walked with Teela, I was aware that I did not fit the many stereotypes of blindness that surrounded me—that a blind woman should stumble and fall, her eyes should look impaired, she should not be able to do things competently and go places on her own; she should be totally blind and not see

1

anything at all. Confronting these stereotypes, I often questioned my legitimacy. Am I really blind? Do I need this dog? But then I would stumble or bump into an obstacle I did not see, lose my way, or feel temporarily helpless. Though distressing, these hazardous moments reassured me of my own form of blindness.

This book, then, is about blindness but not about a stereotype. Ultimately, it is a story about my quest for acceptance of my own ways of seeing and not seeing. *Traveling Blind* is intended both for the general reader and as a contribution to the academic fields of disability studies, feminist ethnography, and the study of human-animal bonds. Beginning with my first sociological work, I have experimented with narrative form, exploring topics in an innovative way that involves the reader and encourages new perspectives as I seek to let others "see" what I see. In an earlier methodological study, *Social Science and the Self*, I argued for the value of a first-person approach to the development of academic knowledge. Rather than viewing the self of the inquirer as a contaminant, I championed the importance of the use of the subjective experiences of an author to inform about larger social processes. I have long had an interest in ways of seeing as well as in what is seen.

Although an intensely personal account, *Traveling Blind* is not simply memoir, for it extends beyond the personal to illuminate our understandings of vision. What does it mean to travel blind? I ask. What is it like to live in an ambiguous world where things are not black and white so much as there and not there, present and absent, shades of gray? What is it like to navigate through constantly changing imagery that requires changing inner perspectives as well? What can experiences of blindness tell us about sight? In the Bibliographic Notes at the end of this book, I provide a suggestion of the rich scholarly literature to which *Traveling Blind* seeks to contribute, including both abstract and personal studies. In these notes, I have focused especially on women's accounts, for too often disability writings tell us primarily about the experiences of men.

For over twenty years, I have been writing and teaching feminist ethnography in a way that emphasizes a personal approach, but only in the past decade have I been significantly losing my eyesight. That experience has challenged me to confront even more honestly than before the realities around me. At a time in my life when I might like to fall back on prior work and habits, I have found I must begin again in terms of learning new skills for reading and writing and for comprehending my experiences, learning to travel blind. It has been a humbling process, causing me to value my own unique ways of seeing and my abilities to be resourceful. In this process, having a guide dog has uplifted my spirits and enabled me to feel less alone. Walking with Teela, I have been prompted to reinterpret the world around me as I navigate it with changed sight. Often I have had to come to terms with contradictions, both within myself and between how I view myself and how others see me.

I am both blind and sighted. I alternately see and fail to see, and I often struggle with my visual impairments. First diagnosed in 1996, my eye condition, called "birdshot retinochoroidopathy," is a rare autoimmune disease that causes inflammation on my retina and choroid and affects both my central and my peripheral vision. The term "birdshot" refers to the scattered lesions in my eyes, said to resemble a spray of birdshot from a gun. Although the severity of the condition—the amount of swelling and scarring—varies over time, the condition is chronic and progressive without a cure. Its symptoms include blind spots, central areas in which I don't see; distortions, such as seeing wavy lines instead of straight ones; color loss; lack of detailed vision; blurriness; darkening of my sight; faulty depth perception; occasional double vision; and large floaters in front of my field of view. I have areas of blindness on the edges of my sight: above and below, left and right. Images look diminished in size, and I am slow to see images and to adapt to visual changes. I see primarily what is straight ahead, and I see pieces of the world one at a time. Objects move into my view, seemingly from out of nowhere, and suddenly I will see them, then lose them again.

My vision loss affects my abilities to read and write and my mobility. This book is unusual in that it focuses on mobility—on my adventures in travel—rather than on more sedentary experiences. My title, *Traveling Blind: Adventures in Vision with a Guide Dog by My Side*, suggests the process of moving through space, constantly asking: What do I see? What don't I see? How do I make sense of it? And how can I navigate with assistance?

Central to all my movements is a concern with my safety. Several years ago, while walking alone, I was hit by a car that I did not see coming because it was in a blind spot in my peripheral vision. I was tossed up on the hood of the car, spun around, and thrown onto the sidewalk. Although I was not badly hurt, I was severely shaken and I vowed to be more careful in the future. I often remind myself of that accident—because the fact that I see some things makes me think I see more than I do. Sight is so dominant a sense that it tends to overwhelm my awareness of my blindness and this can jeopardize my safety.

In *Traveling Blind*, I confront my denials. I speak with as much honesty as I can about the ambiguities of how I see and feel, trying to depict for the reader the excitement of the visual imagery I do see and, at the same time, the nonvisual sounds and smells and, most of all, the "feel" of things.

How does it feel, for instance, to see a simple desert landscape—far more simple than it would look to another person's eye? To see a person's face and then have it disappear, or to have it look strange and not identifiable? How does it feel not to see what is plainly there? Not to be able to drive? To walk with a guide dog? How does it feel to have people ask me questions all the time, to assume at one moment that I am fully sighted, then at the next that I am more blind than I am? How does it feel to be a very private person who suddenly becomes extremely public by virtue of traveling with a large, highly noticeable golden dog? What is it like to navigate through airports and strange towns, to see when I least expect it, to fail to see when I want to? How does it feel to have an invisible disability?

In answering these questions, I depict a world that is not black and white, sighted and not sighted, but that is always a mixture of all the ways of seeing. It is often assumed, for example, that blind people don't see, but in fact, most blind people have some degree of visual sight. The problem is that this sight is impaired or unreliable. Further, no matter what the degree of visual limitation, blind people see, through touch or hearing, or through some combination of residual vision, memory, and intuition, and through living in the world of the sighted. It is often assumed that blind people are very different from sighted people, when it is my experience that we all occupy the same world, but with unique ways of perceiving and navigating within it.

In this book, I seek to combat some of the stereotypes surrounding blindness—particularly the negative assumption that blindness implies incapacity or lack. Instead, I offer an account of mobility and activity, an appreciation for life, and a richness of both visual and emotional imagery. Although I tell my own story, I hope it resonates with the experiences of others. Coming to terms with one's own ways of seeing seems to me an important process whether an individual is sighted or blind. We all embark on journeys that are often unexpected and that require changed dependencies and new ways of seeing—new ways of integrating sight, sound, mind, and feeling.

I have been fortunate in my travels to have had the companionship of an intimate partner, whom I refer to in this book as Hannah. We have been together for the past twenty-nine years, and happily we have become closer since my vision loss. Hannah, like me, is an academic, and although we have long shared many interests, my disability has challenged us to develop new mutual sensitivities. Hannah has been highly adaptive to my needs in our daily life and beyond. In return, I hope I have enriched her world with new adventures. *Traveling Blind* opens with a story about a time when Hannah drove us through the New Mexico desert when I could no longer drive, because she knew how much I wanted to enjoy this part of the country, to appreciate the sights of the desert before they disappeared from my view. Many years ago when I was teaching at the University of New Mexico, I developed a fondness for the high desert, and although I left it for the West Coast and a position at Stanford University, there was something about the bareness, the dryness, the sense of remove, the big sky over rolling plains that always beckoned me.

Thus even when fully sighted, I would lure Hannah back with me to spend time in gentle regions of the Chihuahuan desert. On our earlier trips, between 1982 and 1996, before my vision loss, I enjoyed what I saw, feasting on the varied landscapes with my eyes, discerning the subtle colors—what looked brown at a distance would actually have shades of green, red, and yellow. I prized seeing the details of my surroundings with great clarity— the turquoise moldings on windows of old adobe homes, the particular outlines of golden aspen leaves in the fall, small purple asters growing close to the ground, fine striations of red hills. I remember the first year I noticed my eyesight fading, when I took a walk through a picturesque residential area of Albuquerque with cactus and chamisa gardens surrounding the houses. I kept taking off my glasses, trying to clean them, searching for the clarity I had seen only the year before. During the next few years, my eyesight became more significantly impaired. As this book opens, just two months after I came home with my young guide dog, and feeling excited to be navigating with her, I am embarking with Teela and Hannah on a new trip. I am not sure how much I will be able to see, but I look for ways I can take pleasure in my surroundings and continue to savor my sight, even as it is fading.

Traveling Blind begins with a story of our adventures in a remote area of the southern New Mexico desert during a trip to a mountain called Big Hatchet. This story gradually introduces my blindness and my close relationships as I wake one morning with Hannah next to me, Teela on the floor at my side, a colorful sunrise dawning. I recall my joy in being able to see Big Hatchet Mountain later that day, as well as my frustrations with the blurriness in front of my eyes. Although grounded in a remarkable geographic place, this story is also about my quest for vision, competence, and self-worth. In the second section of the book, Hannah, Teela, and I cross the border into Mexico, where I must cross the border of my blindness as well. I confront my fears and despair, finding lights in my darkness—significant moments that shine despite my loss of sight. I cherish intimacies between Hannah and me, now all the more meaningful for the unusual circumstances we face. I soon take the reader with me as I navigate with Teela the streets of a small desert town aptly named "Truth or Consequences," and as I delight in the magic of Christmas lights viewed with fading sight.

Back home, in Part 3, I explore dilemmas of walking the streets in my neighborhood with my new guide dog, particularly the experience—and the challenge to my identity—of repeatedly being asked, "Are you training that dog?" The reader accompanies me as I travel through airports with Teela and Hannah, surviving security and learning to navigate in a very public realm with much self-consciousness and with only one hand free, the other tightly grasping the handle of Teela's harness.

In the closing section of the book, the three of us revisit the New Mexico desert so that I can recapture sights, sounds, and feelings that are fast receding from my view. We return to Big Hatchet and then spend time in a local bar. Later I strain, against odds, to see the subtle lights of luminarias, those small candles glowing in brown paper bags set outside at Christmastime that represent my ability to value both the darkness and the light. On an early morning walk, I carry a camera, snapping pictures, although I can barely see through the lens. I hope that when I return home, these pictures will show me what I have missed. By the end of our trip and the close of this book, I have come to value my own mixture of blindness and sight and to feel a much-needed acceptance of myself. My relationships with Hannah and Teela have deepened, gaining a new poignance as we find comfort and expanded possibilities together.

The visit to New Mexico that opens *Traveling Blind* occurred in winter 2003, the return trip two years later. The middle section of the book on navigating duality covers the period in between. On each of our visits to the desert, I compared my past with my present and sought to decipher what I was seeing. I have since traveled to these remote places again and I have found that many of the features of the landscape I strain to see have changed. They have been swept away by desert wind and dust and difficult economic times, much like the objects once within my eyesight have disappeared into a larger, murkier background. Yet my memories remain. The mysterious bar in Hachita where Hannah and I once stopped has closed; the vast stretch of wild land surrounding Big Hatchet Mountain, though still rarely visited, is now patrolled intensively by border police. But despite these shifts, the older visions stand as dusty signposts along the way. Like the desert that gradually reclaims its own, my vision has a quality of gradual change in which my efforts to see—to grasp what is before me, and to appreciate my experiences in a positive way—count more than my losses. Rather than a story of moving from light to total darkness or a story of a startling triumph over blindness, mine is a story of subtle changes, of new insights, and of comforts found in shadows and in the spaces between light and dark where clear vision fails.

Although I write of my experiences as a blind woman, this is a surprisingly visual book. As I take the reader on my journeys, visual scenes of desert grasslands, mountains, and mesas jump forth from the pages like snapshots or photos untaken. I describe what I see in greater detail than I might were I able to take my vision for granted, were I able to assume it will be there tomorrow. I often ask Hannah to describe those parts of my surroundings I cannot see so that I can fill in missing pieces of the picture. I appreciate my vision more now that I am blind than I did when fully sighted. I am happier. Though certain details may be absent for me, the larger features of landscapes stand out, making my experiences deeply memorable.

Picture this: We've set out, Hannah and me and my guide dog Teela, on a winter's morning. The sky is clear and blue, the wind chilly. We are in the very southern part of New Mexico near the border. In the distance are mountains. I am standing with my strong twelve-power binoculars in hand, holding them up to my eyes, trying to see, in as much detail as possible, the towering mountain that has drawn me here, Big Hatchet—a "sky island" amidst a vast plain. I look at it and look at it and stare off into the hazy distance toward Mexico. I look at the golden tan earth at my feet and at my golden dog fading into the surrounding landscape, and at the desert scrub, and I look at Hannah, my loving partner by my side, who is shivering in the cold and wondering what we are doing here. And I am exceedingly, unexpectedly happy. Thus begins the adventure that unfolds in *Traveling Blind*. I start with a moment of surprise and joy, an opening to all that follows. For this is a book about not letting blindness destroy happiness or a sense of adventure, about staying the same person and confronting fears while going into the world, and about solving, always solving, the dilemmas that lie ahead.

PART 1: BIG HATCHET

Chapter 1

Starting at Sunrise

Big Hatchet looms in my imagination, a mountain glistening darkly against the desert sky. Lifting my binoculars to my eyes, I see it ahead of me, its broad silhouette topped by a dome and peak. To my right stretch the Little Hatchet Mountains. Between them, far off, shimmering like jewels in the distant sky, are the Sierra Madres of Mexico. I stand in a vast desert basin between these mountain ranges, surrounded by cactus and creosote bush and dust and little else and do not want to leave. This is a story about the day I traveled to Big Hatchet and did not stay long enough. It is also a story about my blindness, and about the particular ways that I see.

I took photographs that day I visited Big Hatchet, as if they would help me remember, or remind me of something hard to grasp. I take them out now, spread them on my desk, and look at them using a strong magnifier. There I am with my guide dog; there's Hannah with our car. There's the tan desert landscape marked by brown scrub, the suggestion of mountains at the horizons. I think I look happy, excited, at peace. What was it that made this place so special to me? What is it about my sight that keeps changing, making each day an unexpected adventure?

The day I visited Big Hatchet was full of reminders of my limited sight. My partner Hannah and I were on a trip in the desert of southwestern New Mexico. The month was December, winter yet not too cold; clear days, winds, a chill. We had spent the night before in a western-style lodge with high wood ceilings, wood floors, a cavernous yet protected feel. I woke early that morning in the dark thinking about the day to come and about my vision: What would I see? What would I miss? Would I enjoy what I saw?

Before rising, I reached down to touch my guide dog Teela, who lay on a blanket on the floor by my side, tied to the bed with a blue nylon leash. A honey-colored dog, in the dark she was but a mass of fur. Hannah lay next to me in the broad bed. I reached to turn off my alarm before it rang, feeling for it on my bedside table. The room was unfamiliar and I was not sure exactly where on the table I had left my talking clock, or the flashlight I still kept by my side at night but rarely ever used anymore. Since going to guide dog school a few months earlier and realizing that other people moved around in the dark finding things and learning their way, I had stopped using my flashlight and, instead, felt my way as I moved, trying to be more aware of my actions physically. I took pride that just the night before I had braved getting out of bed and walking into the bathroom without a flashlight, feeling with my hands for the wall, the door, the light switch inside the adjacent room.

This morning, sunlight was just beginning to seep at the edges of the heavy curtains that hung on the side bedroom windows. I stepped over Teela. I must have given Hannah a brief kiss, as I do every morning when I wake and she is still sleeping, to let her know that I am getting up. "Stay," I said to my dog as I stepped toward the foot of the bed, moving my feet carefully and feeling in front of me with my hands so that I would not bump into the wooden bench at the foot of the bed where I had placed our bags. I wanted to get to the window quickly. I wanted to look out and see if the sun had risen yet and if there was color in the sky.

At the window, I felt behind the curtain and found a set of wooden shutters, then lifted and pulled them out so that I could put my head in close to the glass and take a look. The brightness of the very early morning outside startled me. The sun was on its way but had not yet risen. In the near distance, behind a tree ahead to my left, a patch of rose-red color stood out. I felt overjoyed. I am always glad when I can still see the color of a sunrise.

But the color was covered with a murky coating. I wondered if this was caused by a screen outside the window or if it was the result of darkness within my eyes. Closing the shutters, I stepped toward the back door of our room to go to an outside patio for a better look. There, scarcely dressed, surrounded by pine trees, I stood shivering in the morning cold and looked into the distance. I hoped the red sunrise would now be a brighter, truer color. It was. But my angle of view, different than inside, was not as good. The color began to turn from deep rose-red to orange.

I ran back into the room and searched in my bags for my camera and took it outside, but it had no film. By this time the deep red color was moving to the right and becoming a lighter orange. The moment of the most intense color had passed. I watched the orange spread across the sky. Back inside, I watched again at the window, then closed the curtain. I turned away, disappointed that I had not been able to see the sunrise better or to save it forever in a photograph. At the same time, I felt happy about what I had seen. It was like a good omen, presaging the day to come.

As I packed the car for our trip south that morning, I carried our bags out the back door, stepping cautiously over barely visible rocks that marked the edges of paths. I played Frisbee with Teela in the circular gravel drive in front of the lodge, sometimes throwing her cloth disc off into the desert scrub accidentally and hoping she would not come back covered with cactus prickers. I wanted to tire her before putting her into the car for our day's trip. After playing, now harnessed up, Teela led me to the kitchen in the dark lodge to pick up a lunch I had requested. We would stop for Hannah's lunch on the way because she was allergic to the food the lodge had prepared. Outside, the sun felt warm and the air cool, and there was a brisk wind, but we would be descending in altitude later and I did not think the chill would be a problem. Or I hoped not. I was trying, in my mind, to make everything perfect, hoping the day would turn out well.

As we drove off in the car—Hannah beside me at the wheel, Teela on the back seat—I watched through the window the bare branches of trees by the roadside outlined brightly against the blue winter desert sky. The leafless trees and the shrubs beside them glowed white and a light straw-colored tan, looking delicate and lacy, lending a bare but not austere feeling to the landscape. It was magical, a finely sculpted look—the surrounding fields seen through iridescent bare branches. As I watched, I sensed but did not see the cold. I felt that winter here in the southern high desert was the best time, a time when individuals stand out, when I could stand out against the landscape and not feel overrun by others or by a thickness of activity. The black asphalt road ahead shimmered in the morning sunlight, the roadside marked by those interlaced bare branches of trees and brush through which the sun glistened as if through snow. I noted my surroundings with a grateful eye.

I was not wearing sunglasses as we drove, although the sun was bright and at an angle. I did not need them because the darkness within my eyes provided protection as I peered out as if through inner streaked glass. Because of my impaired vision, I had a sense of blurriness and a sense that things were missing. The scenery seemed to pass by very quickly. I was not sure what I would be able to see as we drove on or when we reached our destination. So I relished and took joy at each step, in almost everything I now saw—the road, the sky, the low juniper and piñon pines sitting like green Buddhas on dry, wheat-like fields. These different pieces of the landscape entered my vision as if by surprise and suddenly I saw them.

We turned south at a junction in Silver City and headed toward Lordsburg. The road began to climb in a gradual ascent. Soon on both sides of the road were low rock formations, no trees; the vista became broader, the road wider, the vast sky overhead seemed lower, as if everywhere touching the ground. Objects were farther away and harder for me to see, more blurred. I asked Hannah what colors the rock banks by the roadside were; they were pink as well as sandy brown, she told me.

I expected that at one point we would ascend to the highest elevation at the back of the Burro Mountains through which we were now passing. But I could not tell exactly where. I strained to see—looking for a sign to a fire road, FR 851, that would tell me when we had reached the vicinity of Burro Peak, but I could not find it. I had seen this fire road on a map the night before while planning our route, though even then I was straining to see, holding the map an inch from my eye, staring through my magnifier at the letters marking towns and roads until these images blurred away. FR 851 kept blurring out of my vision on the map, just as the real fire road now blurred off into the desert sandstone. I am still not sure where Burro Peak was, but somewhere I thought it was there against the sky—a low rocky peak, part of a low mountain range or high mesa.

A few times, I took out my binoculars to try to see the colors of the rocks next to the highway, but I could not focus well because of the speed of the car. Instead, I took out my camera to look through the telephoto lens. The image became very small. Finally, I sat back next to Hannah and let the scenery pass by—the sandy colors, the bright blue overhead. I thought about the blurriness around me and wondered whether I would, in fact, prefer a clearer view. I thought about my many efforts at sight.

"There's still a pull toward the left," Hannah said softly, interrupting my reverie as we drove on. She had noticed the car veering slightly left when she braked and sometimes while steering.

"Let's check on it when we stop for gas in Lordsburg," I offered, wanting to take care of something. Because I do not drive, I often want to do the extras while Hannah is driving so that I will feel useful. We were descending now and soon began traversing a broad desert plain. Lordsburg lay ahead of us, dotting the horizon. Hannah, who hates to get lost, began searching for our exit. "Do you know which one it is?" she asked.

"Describe them to me," I said.

"One exit goes to the right and the other circles over to the left."

I fumbled for my camera to use it to try to find the exit.

"There's no time," Hannah said, turning left.

"Where does the right road go?" I asked.

"Right goes to Arizona." She pointed to a haze in the distance suggestive of mountains.

Turning left, we began circling, winding down beneath the highway and then beneath an overhead railroad trestle, going from bright daylight into a cavernous maze that felt underground. Turned around, we then headed up again and into the sun and dust and toward the sky and signs high on poles in the air. We were deposited off onto the half-shaded morning streets of a half-vacant, dusty old western town that time was passing by.

I liked Lordsburg immediately, perhaps because the town was small and surrounded by an emptiness that allowed me to imagine what I wished—a space to grow, a promise, a separation from intrusion, a new start. This must be the old downtown, I thought, as we drove past garages for farm machinery and truck repair, not what we needed for our car. Then I began seeing storefronts, gray buildings standing tall on the shady side of the street. They held secrets to the town, I thought. I could not see beyond their reflective glass fronts, so I asked Hannah, "What do the signs say? What's in the stores?"

"That one's empty," she said. "That's an old hotel. I don't know if it's still in use." "That's an art store or community center. It's closed." "The sign for that one says 'Pharmacy.'"

I saw only a row of reflective gray glass storefronts running for two or three blocks on one side of a broad empty street paralleling the railroad tracks. The stores sat a foot and a half up on the high sidewalks characteristic of these western desert towns, emphasizing their tallness. I kept wishing there would be a store that I wanted to go into, a reason to stop, but it was morning and we needed to find gas.

The road soon widened, the space stretched out and we moved with speed until a gas station appeared. I got out of the car and walked across the asphalt lot to a glassed-in office, feeling imbalanced because I had not taken Teela or my white cane. I wondered if I looked drunk or blind as I walked, though probably, I thought, nobody seeing me would notice anything unusual. Opening the door to the gas station office, I asked the woman attendant sitting at a desk if she had a tire gauge. I wanted to measure the air pressure in our tires to see if an unevenness was causing the pull Hannah had mentioned.

"I have a gauge," the woman said, "but I don't have air. It won't help you much." She paused. I stood thinking. The woman spoke softly with a Texas drawl that was hard for me to understand.

"Do you know who would have air?" I asked her.

"You might try Gentry's."

"How do I get there?"

"Go back the way you came. Did you come on 10? Then get off when you see the sign for the Best Western. He should have air."

The woman wore glasses and had her hair pulled back and she seemed to me of retirement age, so I wondered why she was working here, and I thought she finally smiled. Everything felt still in that little glass office.

"Thank you," I said, hoping to remember the directions and praying they would make sense to Hannah.

I took the step down carefully from the office onto the asphalt, not wanting to trip, aware of missing my dog. Why hadn't I brought her? I can easily forget I may need her, that I will do better with her aid.

"Do you know which way she means?" I asked Hannah back at the car when I gave her the directions.

"Yes," she said.

I climbed in beside her. The car we were driving was a small sports utility vehicle. It handled like a regular car but put us high up, and since we have a sedan at home, the experience of traveling in the desert in an SUV is exciting for Hannah and me. It was not quite "way out west on horseback," but something close. This was the second trip on which we had rented a sports utility vehicle, and I was pleased that Hannah liked driving it. The upright seat supported her weak back and it enabled me to see out in a panoramic way—with windows four-square all around providing a view that felt exhilarating, extending the limits of my sight.

I could not fully follow how Hannah got us back onto the highway, then off again, under the railroad trestle, up onto streets and around a block to Gentry's gas station. She pulled up to a center island where I got out and walked over to a cubicle in which a man stood at a window collecting money.

"Do you have air and a tire gauge?" I asked him.

"I'm so sorry," he said. "I have air, but no gauge. I lent it to a fellow the other night and he never gave it back. You might try the Exxon."

"Where's that?"

"Over there." He pointed toward a blur.

"How do I get there?"

"You go back to the sign for the motel and you turn left." He seemed to think no further explanation was necessary.

I was very aware that I did not see well enough to feel confident about the directions. I felt confused and amazed that in this scattered town there were so many places to get lost obtaining gas. I also noticed that people kept giving me directions in terms of the location of billboards.

At the third gas station, the wind was blowing fiercely, carrying dust and oily gas station grit. The air felt cold as I walked over to another, dirtier, glassed-in office. The attendant, a small older man, handed me a gauge and pointed toward what I assumed was an air hose on a fueling island.

"I'll do it," Hannah said when I returned to the car, taking the gauge from my hand. "Get inside with Teela and keep warm," she told me. Teela's nose was now pressed against the glass of the back window. She was standing on the seat looking out at me longingly as if we should not have this glass between us.

I assumed Hannah felt it would be easier for her to test and fill the tires than it would be for me, since I would not be able to see the markings on the gauge or the little valves on the tires where the air hose should attach. I knew I could fill the tires by feeling for the valves and by using my magnifier. But I conceded. I stood and watched Hannah go and get the air hose from on the ground somewhere out of my sight, pull it over and start to fill the tires. She then re-measured the first tire with the gauge. The pressure was less than it had been before. "It's taking the air out," she said.

I went back to the office to tell the station attendant that the air hose wasn't working. He began to argue, then mumbled something in Spanish that I did not comprehend.

"Come out," I gestured. "Would you try it?"

He knelt down next to the right front tire, attached the hose. "It's not working," he said. Then he went back inside.

A while later, he returned to tell us that the compressor wasn't working. It had been turned off the night before and hadn't been turned back on yet. We should wait for fifteen minutes and let it warm up and then we could fill the tires.

Hannah did most of the work. I assisted. I watched her kneel down with one knee on the ground while attaching the air hose. I was worried that the knee of her light-colored pants would get dirty, but she did not seem to mind. I kept thinking about how I used to be the one to fill our tires, but now I just helped. With my hands, I felt for and found the air valves on the tires, invisible up under the body of the car. And I gave advice.

We filled the tank up with gas. When we drove off, although the air pressure in the tires was now even, the pull to the left was still discernable, so I figured it was probably built into the car. The theme of things "not working" struck me. I thought it must be typical of Lordsburg—having to go to three stations to get air, the wind blowing, things broken and missing. I thought, too, about my eyesight and about how parts of it are not working—how part of what I see is always missing, while other aspects stand out in remarkable detail, such as the delicacy of bare trees in the morning sunlight, or the contours of the ground in three different gas stations. Perhaps I was more detail-oriented now because of my broken eyesight. The objects I still could see meant more to me than before and I seemed to need to know more specifics about my surroundings in order to get my bearings.

"I can see it from here," Hannah said suddenly.

I looked out the car window and up at a billboard for the Best Western Skies Motel and for Kranberry's Family Restaurant. The restaurant stood a stone's throw from the billboard, next to the Best Western, and diagonally across from the Exxon. It was a low, modern building with broad windows. We pulled into the parking lot where I put Teela's harness on her, and with her guiding me, I walked with Hannah up the pathway to the front door, trying not to feel conspicuous. Inside, while Hannah ordered a takeout lunch, I stepped over to a mock covered wagon that held a display of tourist items—decorative tiles, postcards, ceramic red chiles. I handled several black baseball hats that said "Kranberry's," thinking, would I wear one? Would people then ask, "Where's Kranberry's?" How would I answer, how would I explain my travels?

Hannah came over and we entered the restrooms. As I exited, I walked out past startled women and children who exclaimed loudly upon seeing that a dog had suddenly appeared from within a bathroom stall. I waited for Hannah in a narrow hallway outside the restrooms where paintings hung on the walls—small framed watercolors and oils, miniature landscapes, many of them in blue tones. They hung against a backdrop of striped green wallpaper. I walked up to one painting, then another, and put my head close to the glass to see the features—a tree, a distant mountain—then I stepped back. I took out my small round pocket magnifier to help me see better, holding it up close to the paintings, but then the watercolors blurred into indefinable forms. A label said this was an exhibit of the Art Society of Lordsburg. I marveled that an art show was hanging here on walls outside restrooms next to an ice machine in a restaurant off the interstate.

Hannah soon joined me looking at the paintings; she described some of them to me, then she went to pick up her lunch. While she paid at the desk, I sat on a bench in the lobby near the front door, Teela beside me. A woman came over, and seeing Teela, began talking to me about her dog who had died; she was not over it. As I listened to her, I thought I should get used to people telling me about their dogs. Having Teela with me stirred their feelings. There was much for me to learn about traveling with a guide dog—I definitely felt more accessible in public; people talked to me more. Hannah returned with her lunch in a box. She checked out the covered wagon. A CD by a local woman caught her eye, a collection of "Cowboy Songs." Before purchasing it, she made sure it had at least one song about a cowgirl. With music to accompany our drive, we were on our way.

As we left Lordsburg, the landscape began to change, only hinting at what lay ahead. We were now driving farther south, and just outside town, we passed what seemed to me to be a lake or large pond. How could water be here? I wondered. Was it water or a dry basin that looked like water? Hannah was concentrating on her driving in order not to get lost. "I'll look later," she said when I asked her to be my eyes.

I had a vague feeling that I had read that birds could sometimes be sighted on the flats south of Lordsburg, and perhaps the water was the reason. I took out my camera to look through the telephoto, but I could not figure out what I was seeing.

As we drove on, the water receded into plains and a new kind of flatness. The earth stretched white in all directions, the sun glistening off it, enveloping us in a hazy light. The mountains in the distance seemed far away, buildings infrequent. This was arid ranchland, or what once was ranchland—sparse vegetation, almost bare. Things were lying around, but nothing seemed clearly to announce what it was. A barbed wire fence extended indefinitely, a row of trees faded into dry fields, a sign saying "Hill" was followed by a slight incline. Occasional signs announced upcoming towns that you could drive through without knowing that you had missed them.

"Let's stop," I said to Hannah, seeing several buildings and a dirt parking lot beside the road, along with signs Hannah read for a post office and a cafe. I wanted to get out and see my surroundings close up, feel the ground at my feet, gain my bearings. I hoped perhaps to go into the cafe for a sense of local color, get a lunch, though I already had one, buy something, as if that would tell me I was here.

A small, hand-painted sign above the door to a modest rear building read, "Cafe and General Store." As I entered guided by Teela, who followed Hannah, a wooden screen door knocked shut behind me. I stepped past several long tables covered with white oilcloths, past posters announcing an upcoming potluck. The smell of fried cooking grease hung in the air. A window in back of the one-room cafe let in a few streams of sunlight. No one seemed to be around.

I knew the burnt grease odor would bother Hannah, that she would want to leave quickly, but the odor made me wish to stay, to order an item of local cooking, maybe Mexican. I walked over to investigate a glassed-in counter in the back of the room, thinking this must be the general store component. I put my eyes down close to the glass to try to see the items on the shelves beneath it, but I could not make them out—some small boxes that looked blurred. I wondered if there was another room next door but that was probably the post office.

A woman appeared and stepped behind the counter to wait on me. I asked her if there might be another general store nearby, as if to explain my close scrutiny of the items. Then a man, a local, I think, walked in and began talking with the woman. I wished, right then, that I was a local. I wished I could see the items in the display. I wished Hannah did not have allergies and get headaches from closed-in burnt grease. I wished I could sit at a table and order food and take in the place and pretend, just pretend for a while that I lived here—in the middle of seemingly nothing where the land stretches, where towns exist but are not visible, where things glow white and shimmering tan, and far away are Mexico, Arizona, industries and railroads. Clearly now, I felt, we were on our way; we were leaving family restaurants for the south, for new vistas and possibilities.

The name of the town we had stopped in was Animas, for "spirit." I liked the poetic sound of the name and the sense of a spirit matching the landscape and my expansive hopes for my own life. Some miles later, we passed through another small town, which also had a cafe, but we did not stop. I wanted to, but there were two of us, and how often could I walk into a murky interior looking for something I might not find, that perhaps was not even there—good food, recognition, a community life in which I could feel special and enjoy a new comfort in being, perhaps a new reconciling with my blindness.

Before we left the Animas Cafe, the woman at the counter had given me directions to where there might be another general store. She pointed toward the front door and mentioned a hill ahead and a road to the left that climbed a little and said there was a store over there, if they were open or still in business.

As we drove on now, I kept looking for the hill and the road up, though I never saw it. Hannah seemed to think she did, but the landscape was hazy, glistening as if with wet sun, and things were not what they seemed.

We turned east at Route 9, listening to the cowboy music on the car stereo—stories of a woman's love for men, which felt oddly out of place in our car. But the female singer was soulful, the music rich, and I kept waiting for the subject to shift to love of cowgirls.

Chapter 2

Finding Big Hatchet

Wide vistas now extended on both sides of the road. My view was of whiteness—hazy, blurry whiteness—interrupted by fences, the suggestion of brown, a low mountain range in the distance. The landscape was so phantomlike I worried about whether I would be able to see anything well as we continued on. I seemed to be taking us into a land of invisibility, where I might not see what I had come for.

This trip to the Bootheel was planned especially for me. It was my day to take us somewhere I had long wanted to visit. Many years ago when I taught at the University of New Mexico, I had wanted to go south to the Big and Little Hatchet Mountains and to visit the town of Hachita. These places were far away and viewed as desolate; only a few people went there. Friends wondered why I wished to go. Back then, I tended to take off on trips to the countryside by myself and I was often lonely. Now I had Hannah with me. Ever since I met her, over twenty years ago, I had a fantasy that we would be on the road together, the two of us bumming around. We had only fulfilled my fantasy in short bursts—trips to New Mexico and to the California coast—but the fantasy was still with me. Now with my eyesight fading, Hannah wanted to be sure to take me places she knew I wished to see. I wanted to make sure that, at the same time, we did what she liked.

Yesterday was her day. We spent it in Silver City where Hannah had a lazy morning, played music, and later had a massage at a health spa high on a hill. While she was having her massage, I walked the nearby streets with Teela but was disappointed that I could see so little—even in people's front yards—that I feared getting lost. So I came back to the spa and sat on a couch surrounded by candles and the scents of essential oils. I took out my maps and magnifiers to go over our route for today.

Driving now through open country, I looked out the car window at the whiteness around me and saw less well what lay before my eyes than the pictures I had in my mind. Particularly, I saw the tiny town of Hachita, toward which we were headed. I recalled photographs from a magazine that I had looked at through my magnifier many times when deciding on our destination. The photos had bright colors and the quality of the light within them suggested they were taken in the early morning or late in the day, when the light was soft and magical. There were brown tones, rosy yellow highlights, a bright blue sky against which lone buildings were clearly defined: a white church, a brown barn with a man in front of it. A window frame stood alone on a hillside embedded in an eroded adobe structure—what was left of a house now gone. The sky, seen through that window, looked intensely blue. The picture of it was taken in Old Hachita, a town eventually abandoned for Hachita, but still up there somewhere on a hill. I thought we might enjoy visiting the old and new town, perhaps even more than arriving at Big Hatchet. I wanted to see in real life what I had seen in the colorful magazine pictures.

As we drove on, a low peaked mountain range appeared against the silvery blue sky. I held the map up for Hannah to see so she could identify it. "The Little Hatchets," she said. A slight hill came into sight and then a sign for Hachita, eight miles ahead.

I was anxious with anticipation. I had already put a good deal of work into this remote town. Beyond looking at the pictures and article in the magazine, I had inquired further and learned there was a boarding house in Hachita, where I hoped we might spend the night. I made calls trying to locate it but failed. I had also tried to pin down the location of a restaurant. But the Egg Nest, like Larson's Boarding House, seemed a thing of the past, swept away as if by desert winds and dust, never to be seen again. The closest I came to finding places to stop in Hachita was the name of a bar. But the Hachita Tavern, which had possibly become the Hachita Liquor Saloon between the time the article I read was written and the time I sought to track it down, had a phone that just rang and rang. I assumed I was calling at an off hour, or so I hoped. I did not want to let go of my fantasy of Hannah and me sitting in a wooden booth in the bar overhearing Big Joe behind the counter recounting the local news with another man, a rancher. And we'd order hamburgers and have a drink and go upstairs to our room in Larson's, perhaps now missing because attached to the bar. Trips to such places are often made not once but many times, I have found, most of them in fantasy, yet each with its own kind of indelible reality.

We were now approaching Hachita, though the landscape did not change much. We were on Route 9. Beyond Hachita, this road hugs the border of Mexico and New Mexico, and the surface of the road, from what I had heard, becomes unreliable—sometimes covered with dirt or washed out, the pavement irregular. It was not advised to drive straight through on 9, but instead to go north to I-10, the interstate highway that went through Lordsburg, and then go east to Deming and head south. Here at Hachita, if you turned south, you did not immediately hit the border, but instead entered a vast square of land known as the Bootheel. Hachita was the only town in the north central Bootheel. Forty-six miles south through the desert plains lay Mexico, and between here and there was Big Hatchet.

A Bureau of Land Management representative had told me on the phone that if I drove straight south from Hachita, in ten miles I would find a place with Big Hatchet on the left and the Little

Hatchets on the right, where we could pull the car off the road and walk around. I was looking forward to finding that spot, but I was not sure if Hannah might first want to explore the town.

She was driving rather quickly. I noticed something go by in a blur. "What do you see?" I asked Hannah.

"Just some buildings, a store."

"Stop!" I said. "You're about to pass through Hachita."

She turned right on a street leading toward houses.

"Why are you pulling up here?" I asked her.

"I thought we could have our lunch. It seemed a good spot."

"But I want to go back to the town."

"This is the town."

"I mean where the stores are."

She drove us back over to a parking area off the main road, pulling the car up next to a wooden, barnlike building that appeared to be on stilts, its windows and door boarded up. I wondered if it was the town tavern. Maybe it was open only at night.

"Are you sure you want to stop here?" Hannah asked me.

I looked around. It seemed to me we were surrounded by asphalt—partially paved, part dirt. Ahead of us, some rusted cars and trucks sat in the sun. Beyond them were fences, backyards of homes, clothes on a line. To the left of our car was the boarded-up building. I was beginning to think the spot scenic when Hannah asked again, "Are you sure?"

"What's wrong with it here?"

"We're looking at garbage. Ahead of us are trash cans and things people have dumped."

But I couldn't see it, and we had already moved the car once. So there we had our lunch—the back of the car facing the road and behind it an abandoned railroad track bed, barely visible against the desert plains around it, the front windshield toward the sky and some blurry local features.

After we ate, I got out and walked around with Teela. There

was a wind and everything looked hazy to me and almost indistinguishable from the larger landscape of dusty fields. I could not see the junk Hannah had described, which felt fine to me; but I also could not see the colors or clear silhouettes of buildings that I had seen in the magazine photographs. The stores we had passed on the way in were not far, perhaps forty yards away, but my eyes could not focus on them.

Faced with my lack of sight, I cried inside in a way that matched the fog I saw outside. I felt impatient to get on with things and sad that Hannah and I liked being in different kinds of places. How would I ever work out the day so we each could be happy? I thought of the boarded-up tavern standing weathered behind me, clear in my sight because it was close and large. I wished more of the town was clear. I felt confused.

I got back in the car and we drove over to the buildings at the farther end of the lot, hoping to use a restroom. A small, white establishment had a sign in front that said, "Cafe & Store." Inside, the smell was again of cooking grease, though more faint than in the Animas Cafe earlier, suggesting the cooking had been done a longer time ago. The Hachita Cafe seemed to be a side room off someone's house; it had a few tables covered with blue oilcloths near the front windows; a hallway in back, which served as the store, had utilitarian items for sale—sterno, matches, soap. I looked around for something to buy so that Hannah might ask the favor of our using the restroom. A woman came out to help us.

"What flavors are these?" I asked her, pointing to a stack of muffins on a table, toward which Teela's nose was directed. I chose one blueberry and one chocolate chip muffin, each wrapped for posterity in plastic. Hannah then asked the woman if she could use the bathroom.

"It's not working," the woman said apologetically. "You might try next door." She pointed left.

Outside, I wanted to walk over to where the woman had pointed, since it was not far, but Hannah discouraged me. The asphalt was broken and she feared I would not see the breaks and would trip, even with Teela guiding me.

We backed the car up and drove over to a larger building that said "STORE" in bold, painted letters. Two gas pumps sat out front, though it was not clear if they were working. Near them stood a rack of black ponchos decorated with huge silver horses; a sign above them read, "Ponchos, $20." A friend had asked me to bring her back a poncho from our travels. I had told her I was not sure I would find one. "You don't find them just blowing in the wind by the roadside," I had said. But here was a rack, and indeed they were blowing. Yet I didn't think she would wear a huge silver horse rearing up on its hind legs. She was a small woman. I wanted to get her something more tasteful. Perhaps there would be more inside.

I followed Teela up a step and opened the front door of the Hachita Store. Inside, shelves with candy sat beside a cash register on my right, shelves on aisles stretched to the rear with household items and packaged foods: cereal, canned milk, soda, soup; two video game machines stood next to a lottery ticket booth by the front window, beside them a counter with coffee pots and two tables. Near the tables, a set of tall black shelves displayed cheap Mexican tourist items—pink and lime green ashtrays, little figures of painted animals, a stack of more ponchos with the horse, most of them black but some magenta, green, and yellow. Someone had gotten a surplus shipment of those ponchos, I thought.

Hannah asked to use the restroom. I bought a roll of Life Savers, not feeling as big a spender this time. When Hannah returned, she struck up a conversation with the woman proprietor at the counter.

"Where's Route 81 heading south?" she asked, seeking to get her bearings.

"Just up ahead," the woman responded.

"And Old Hachita?"

"It's five miles back on your left, where you see the hill. You should go there. It's nice." The woman also suggested, because she had noticed my fingering the ponchos, that if we were looking for a gift we should continue on Route 9, since we should be able to find some better ones in Mexico.

"Route 9?" Hannah asked.

"I heard Route 9's not a good road between here and Columbus?" I ventured.

"It's fine," the woman said. "People drive it all the time. Only the last five miles are slow."

"Maybe Mexico," Hannah murmured to me as we stepped out of the store. I think she wanted to please me, to make our trip feel exotic, something I'd remember.

"I don't know," I said. "Let's go to Big Hatchet."

The road south from Hachita seemed nondescript at first. I was going away from something, but I could not tell what I was going to. It was exciting for me to think that somewhere ahead lay Mexico—a place I have wished to visit since childhood. I have associated it in my mind with color, adventure, and people living their lives fully. Not far south of Hachita, the Little Hatchet Mountains came into view once more—a low, gray range with jagged peaks. We seemed to be passing them, but they stayed in sight in the west. I felt we were descending in elevation, though the surrounding plains remained flat and increasingly they looked less strictly white, more brownish in tone. They were dotted with brown scrub—aged cactus, dry brittle bush. I wanted to identify the plants beside the road, but they looked blurred. I was tilting my head, trying to get their outlines clear, when a second mountain came into view, a gray mass, small at first against the southeastern horizon. I smiled.

"Big Hatchet," I said to Hannah. I felt happy, as if I hadn't expected to find it. I took out my binoculars. Although a mountain is large, it is small and hazy in my sight and I wanted not to miss it. I wondered where the pull-off would be. Hannah looked at her odometer to check our mileage. Just then, in the midst of a stretch of extending desert, the road widened. Perhaps millions of years ago, an ocean lay here or a vast lake, bounded now by these "sky islands"—the Little Hatchet range to the west, a smaller peak and the mountaintops of Mexico glimmering in the south, and Big Hatchet itself, looming like a giant shadow. I liked how this place, though vast, had a sense of boundedness. Big Hatchet grew larger as we approached it, feeling both close and far away at the same time—beckoning, dramatic.

Hannah pulled the car off onto a dirt side road that cut into the main road from our left and that seemed to extend eastward and somewhat north of Big Hatchet. We parked amidst dust and tall scrub. I was excited and afraid. I had visions of bandits driving by in vans and stopping to loot our car when we left it to take a walk. Hannah, however, did not seem worried. Perhaps for her, parking near the main road offered security. I wanted to drive farther on the dirt road, hide the car, and get out and walk around where nobody would see us. I think Hannah did not imagine we would walk far. I had not expected to find a road here. The man at the Bureau of Land Management had not mentioned one. The mountain glistened.

I almost tumbled out of the car, so quickly did I want to get my bearings and see if I liked the place. I grabbed my binoculars and held them up to my eyes, as if fearing the mountain would disappear. But there it stood, a huge mound with a dome on top, and next to the dome, a peak. It did look like a big hatchet laid on its side. I stared at it through my binoculars for a long time, for so long that, after a while, a magnification of twelve times normal seemed to me the real view. The mountain I saw with my naked eye paled by comparison. When I lowered my binoculars, the desert plain again filled my field of vision, dwarfing Big Hatchet and the other mountains. I took out my camera from the glove compartment in the car, hung it around my neck along with my binoculars, put my hat on for shade, and bundled up. Teela, beside me, sensed my excitement, wagged her broad tail, perked up her ears, and was especially alert. Hannah, Teela, and I started off on a walk.

The dirt road ahead seemed newly cut out of the surrounding desert. The sides of it went straight up, as if they had not had time yet to erode away. I felt that with some turns, this flat road would eventually lead to Big Hatchet, as if with a few steps more, or a few steps beyond that, just up ahead past a curve in the distance, there it would be.

I kept picking up my binoculars to look at it. I was overjoyed to see it. The mountain looked dark gray, almost black, and hazy as if covered with a sugary glaze. It had a distinct swollen hatchet shape. At one point, it looked bright blue. I had once seen an artist's silkscreen print of a mountain, huge and blue, and I had wondered, why paint a mountain blue? It seemed unnatural, but here it was in real life.

The light on the mountain changed as we walked alongside it and as I switched from my naked eye to my binoculars, to my camera, and back to my naked eye, until I could not tell what reality was—some combination of these lenses, these different clarities and brightnesses, sizes, and colors. With my twelve power binoculars, I saw color strongly; without them, color faded. My camera, at four power, was weak compared to my binoculars, but it enlarged more than my eyes, which were glary and dark at the same time. They bathed the scene in a wash as if I was seeing it under water. I used one eye, then the other; the left was sharper. My eyes took in the mountain and the desert.

"You're not thinking we'll walk all the way there," Hannah said to me. "It's windy. I'm cold out here."

The sun was shining. I wasn't cold. I was too excited. But the wind made the air brisk.

I was indeed thinking that we would walk all the way there, unrealistic as that was. Hannah went back to the car to put on more clothes, leaving Teela and me to continue. Then she drove over and parked near us farther down on the dirt road. She would walk some more.

I raised my camera. "Let's take a picture," I said. I focused on the mountain, which looked smaller than in my binoculars, smaller than it should. But it was the best I could do. I took a picture of Big Hatchet; I took the Little Hatchet range. I took a picture trying to see all the way down to Mexico. I took Teela glowing gold, excited yet patient; I took Hannah buried in her hat. I took a sign that said "Hatchet Wildlife Area." I wanted to be reminded, to remember, fearing I'd forget. I hoped my pictures would show something I could not now see with my eyes. Maybe later I would look at them and find it and suddenly my life would be changed. I knew the mountains would look small in a photograph, but there they would be.

I wondered what this dirt road was doing here; it looked so recent. There were tire tracks, but I felt we were the only ones ever to come here, ours were the only footprints, now fast being blown away.

I pointed my binoculars and then my camera at the desert scrub near the road to try to identify the plants. But even with my binoculars in close focus and my camera on autofocus, the cactus and brush looked blurry. They did not look like recognizable plants, more like stringy, fuzzy shapes. My eyes made them murky and undefined. I never could get them clear and I could not understand why my visual aids would not help me. Hannah pointed out a bush that looked reddish, but I could see no color; she pointed to something that might be, or once had been, a flower, but I could not see it, and I wanted to.

I thought maybe if I got off the road and walked in among the cactus, I would be able to discern the plants better. I tried a little. I climbed up, leaving Teela with Hannah, and took a few steps alone among the plants, but I feared bumping into cactus that I could not see, so I did not go far. I had trouble focusing on even the closest bush, as if the combination of bright light reflecting off dust, spreading everywhere from an overhead glassy blue-silver sky, was too much for my eyesight to comprehend.

Big Hatchet, however, was defined. It blocked the glare, captured it, stood between me and blindness in a way I had not at all expected.

"We can come back," Hannah said, as if reading my mind.

"But I'm not all here yet."

We now walked slowly, then quickly on the dirt road and I took in my surroundings many times over. Big Hatchet looked down, guarding the desert protectively. I was more secure with the car parked farther away from the main road. I was surprisingly secure. I didn't feel as if I did not belong here. There was no sense of local color that I was missing, though I did feel the mountain was just beyond my reach. I had seen, long ago in a picture, a surface of craggy rocks with desert bighorn sheep climbing up them that were probably in the blackness of the mountain I saw ahead. Up close, Big Hatchet was bound to be rugged and difficult. But I was not thinking of climbing it. Looking at it was my challenge.

"Do you want to get in the car and drive further?" Hannah asked. "But remember, I don't know if this road leads there. Next time, we'll bring a map."

How could it not lead to Big Hatchet? I wondered, as if all roads in this vicinity would go there.

We drove on the dirt road and eventually it took a curve, then led straight again. If farther away there was a turn south toward Big Hatchet, it was not to be seen.

"Only for you, dear," Hannah said smiling, looking over at me as she drove, grasping the steering wheel tightly. I was touched by her willingness to brave lost directions, wind and chill, and a sense of barrenness in an unknown borderland. I was touched by her statement that we could come back, even as I did not want to leave. Coming back might not be the same. It might never happen. I had not explored enough yet, hadn't seen enough. I raised my binoculars to take the scene with me, enfold it with my eyes—the array, the desert, the mountains at the peripheries—the Little Hatchets, the Sierra Madres, Big Hatchet. Why was everything a hatchet around here? What happened out in this desert at night? What would happen when I left?

Hannah wanted to go back and I wanted to stay. I knew we had not planned a full day's trip to Big Hatchet. I had not expected for certain that we would come here. But once here, I worried that in the future, I would not see well enough to return. I still would not be able to drive. If only I could drive, I thought, I could go home and come right back. But that would be by myself, like I used to be, not with Hannah. Though this day was planned for me, it was also with her. I did not want to go back to that previous time in my life before I knew Hannah, when I was lonely. I had more fun now; I felt special when with her, less fearful, and happier than before.

"We're together, that's the most important thing," Hannah would often say to me. "What's most important?" she would insist on my answering.

And my answer would be clear and the same each time: "Loving, that's the most important thing."

"And?"

"Being together. You and me together. And Teela."

"I promise you, we'll come back. Just say the word."

We drove slowly, returning to the place where the dirt road met the main road. The day was getting cooler, the afternoon later, the light changing, becoming slightly less bright. At the entrance to the paved road, Hannah parked the car. I got out and knelt with Teela next to the Hatchet Wildlife Area wooden sign so Hannah could take our picture. I wanted this picture of my dog with me, a picture that would say I was here. I never expected the photo would turn out well, but it did and I saw myself—my eyes looked steady and glowing, my arm around Teela. I stood then and looked in all directions. I snapped a picture of Hannah that cut off the top of her head, for peering through the camera's viewfinder, I could not see her as well as I could see Big Hatchet.

I was never really at Big Hatchet, I suppose. I was in that

stretch of desert surrounding it. I was not somewhere else. I was not in a town. I was walking around taking in the sights with my patient guide dog and the car that I could not drive and with my beloved Hannah.

I had wanted to keep walking and get all the way to Big Hatchet and spend the night—camp out in a cabin like one I had seen in a photo, which, in my imagination, combined with an image of a bearded old man who lived there. I would stay at the foot of the rough-hewn mountain and feel protected and different and far away from people who might judge me as lacking. I would stay by the mountain and not have to confront what I don't see or can't be. I would hear the desert bighorn sheep and the coyotes and the javelinas at night. I'd see them, too, with my binoculars. I'd drive up to Hachita to eat. I'd come back.

But I did not know if I would come back. The desert surrounding Big Hatchet is desolate and far away and my eyesight keeps changing. Why make Hannah drive? A trip here clearly is not a massage or a day soaking in hot mineral water in the sun. It's not the two of us naked; it's us all bundled up, braving only slightly harsh elements. Consider this desert in the summer sun—searing, windy, uninhabitable. No wonder the scrub was brown and unseeable.

"Goodbye, Big Hatchet," I thought with sadness as we drove off. I was angry at Hannah for wanting us to leave. I felt angry at my fate. I was unhappy. The one place I wanted to come, and now I had to go.

Yet I knew there were two of us. I would not be here but for Hannah. I had not actually come before by myself. Maybe some places are too desolate, too remote, better visited in company. I am still sifting it over in my mind. If I saw better, would I have enjoyed Big Hatchet as much? What if I saw less? We had walked on that sandy tan dirt road, and I had looked around with my binoculars and I saw what I could see, what reassured me. And we were not robbed, and I did not fall, and I did not get stung by cactus. Then we drove back on Route 81, that north-south strip of road, asphalt but patchy, leading from a spot seemingly nowhere in particular, but scenic enough for a Bureau of Land Management representative to tell me about it, and for a sign that led to a road branching to the left toward a mountain alive in my mind as Big Hatchet.

I never liked mountains much before, or had any special affection for them, but now I did, at least for this one. Yet I felt so sad. We were driving back toward Hachita and all I wanted to do was to turn the car around.

"We'll come again," Hannah said, reaching her arm over and touching my shoulder to reassure me as we drove.

Chapter 3

Leaving with Regrets

The light overhead seemed darker than before, dusk was approaching. At Hachita, we parked in front of a church that I thought I had seen in the magazine photos. But when I looked up at it, I could not get an angle from which to see it well, or it was too dark, or I was too tired, or too used to seeing mountains. I thought perhaps this was not the same church as in the magazine. It seemed darker, more odd; maybe there was another church, or the photographer took his picture on a sunnier day; mine was bleak and confusing.

"We can try looking for another church," Hannah offered in good spirits. She was glad, I think, to be on our way back.

I thought she might like to see more of the town. We decided to give Hachita one more chance before leaving. We would drive over to Old Hachita. Stopping first for directions at the Hachita Store with the gas pumps and ponchos out front, we headed back on Route 9 for the seven miles it actually took to reach the hill where the abandoned town was said to lie. Hannah turned off the road where she saw an unmarked metal gate on our left.

I got out and pulled it open so she could drive through. The gate looked new; it was still shiny. We started driving up a hill that felt like we were on the side of a small cliff. As we got higher, the road clung closer to the edge of the cliff. The dirt surface looked red and hard, with deep ruts, a split in the middle. Hannah drove steadily around potholes. Afraid of heights, I felt in danger here. I looked for the old town but saw only this winding road, rutted as if an earthquake had come and split open parts of it. As we rounded a curve, I thought that perhaps Big Hatchet would be visible in the distance from our higher vantage point. But it seemed lost in the desert below.

The road became rougher and we never got to Old Hachita. After a time of tense driving, I asked Hannah how she would feel about turning around.

"Fine," she said. "I was only going because I thought you wanted to. I want you to feel better."

"But I wanted to come for you, so you could see something you'd like. You said you wanted to see a ghost town."

"I've seen enough ghost towns."

She turned the car around on the narrow road while I closed my eyes and held my breath, relieved when we were again back in sight of the steel gate. I pulled it open and Hannah parked outside it. I took out Teela's food bowl, laying it on the ground near the gate. She was hungry and lapped up her meal gratefully. Behind me, the ascending road led, I imagined, to a window frame standing alone on a hillside, to homes once inhabited, a few discarded utensils, dishes left over from a time before the railroad came when a town nestled protectively up in these hills.

Occasional cars drove by on Route 9. I wondered how other people managed to drive the road behind the gate and get to Old Hachita. I thought about places I hadn't been that were beyond my reach or sight. I thought about Hannah and me traveling together, wanting to please each other.

We headed back toward Hachita to take a road north. I was aware that nothing could really quiet my sadness. As we passed through the town, the storefronts flashed by outside my window in a blur. I looked to my right: maybe the tavern would be open now, maybe people would be in it and we could go in too. I thought about asking Hannah to stop so I could see my surroundings better. But I did not ask and we didn't stop. Inside I was flowing with tears of grief and not wanting to admit it. Why did I have to leave Big Hatchet? Leaving has always been hard for me, but my losses seem more final since my eyesight has faded, for I fear I will not see as much if I return.

I have an image of Hannah driving us on the straight road north. The sky is bright gray; it's a late winter's afternoon, the sun low by 4 p.m. We had already turned at the junction in Hachita and were miles along on our route, on a faster road back than the one we had taken in, when I was struck by the import of what I had not seen. I wished, with a sudden inner pang of regret, that I had asked Hannah to stop in the town once more and to describe for me everything she saw—the colors, the details, what the storefronts looked like; what exactly was the garbage I hadn't seen earlier? What was across the street? What could she tell me so I could fill in more sharply the fuzzy picture I saw, the picture I was missing? Even more, I wished I had taken a photograph in Hachita—of where I had been and what I had seen only hazily—so that later I could take it out and see the cafe, the parking lot, the surrounding plains with a sharpness I had not had at the time. I wanted to see as clearly in my pictures what I had seen in the magazine photos, though I wanted my own version.

I had not missed seeing with clarity at Big Hatchet in the broad open desert, but I did miss it in the town, where detail was supposed to be visible, where I had an image in my mind that did not match what I could fill in with my eyes. That I saw Hachita in my own way—ephemeral, ghostlike, blurred, a dusty stop on the road through to Mexico, or if you turned south, to Big Hatchet— seemed not the point. If only I had taken a picture, if only Hannah had told me.

The eyes are viewed as telling, as reliable, as providing a sense of really having been there, a sense felt as most true when it is most sharp, when, in fact, that is not so. They are one door, one entry. I have told myself this over and over, but I mourned the detail I missed.

We drove on, leaving Hachita with its houses and store and ponchos blowing in the wind, and a boarded-up tavern and possibly a boarding house waiting for a nighttime crowd.

We headed now through broad plains, remnants of overgrazed ranchland. The fields beside the road looked vacant, lacking in vegetation. This wasn't the same barren land as near Big Hatchet, where the desert was parched but full of cactus and scrub. It was whiter here, more bare. I looked around and wondered if I was missing something.

"What do the plants you see look like?" I asked Hannah, as I had done so many times on this day.

"Not like much. Here." She popped her CD into the car stereo where the singer's tone was reminiscent of my own, the strains of her tune mixing Mexican mariachi music with nostalgia for these desert plains.

I wanted to explain my sadness to Hannah. It was certainly no way to reward her for having taken me so far. "I think I'm sad because I want to feel special," I told her. "I feel I have to go far away to a place where no one else goes to be special. I'm afraid people won't value me."

And she smiled in that way she has of seeming to know more than I do.

"I'll take you back," she said. "But you don't have to come all the way here to be special. You're special for me always. I wish I could make you feel that."

"Thank you," I said.

"I like being on the road together, you and me," Hannah added.

The drive north seemed to go on forever, a time for thought. Behind me, Teela lay curled up sleeping comfortably on the rear seat, her presence reassuring. Eventually we reached I-10, the interstate that would lead us back west through Lordsburg. It was a jolt. Huge trucks lumbered by. Too quickly, I was leaving behind a quieter place.

Soon after we turned onto the interstate, a log cabin-shaped building came into view, topped with a sign that said, "Trading Post." Someone had told me to look for it in our search for a better poncho. We made the stop. Feeling otherworldly, I walked with Hannah and Teela up a ramp and into a store that stretched broadly left and right with wooden floors and shelves stocked with Mexican and American tourist items and hobby supplies—rugs, jewelry, housewares, clothing, stuffing for pillows, glitter, paint, decorated pots, birdhouses, curios of all kinds. We went straight over to a counter piled high with dusty ponchos made out of Mexican blankets. Hannah tried on a few to see how they would look on our friend, but they simply looked like a blanket thrown over a small person.

I wanted to search further in the store—for a gift for my sister, or for myself, and to see what was around. Hannah followed me, watching out so I would not bump into anything and so I could ask her advice about colors. I picked up a shoulder bag and asked what she thought of it. "Too chintsy," she said. "It's really cheap looking."

I handled rugs and blankets. At one point, I showed Hannah a placemat with a cactus and a mountain on it that I was considering purchasing for my sister. Hannah looked at me. "I feel really sad," she said. "The things you're picking up. You can't see, but they are terrible. They are in very bad taste, and you don't know it. You never would have looked at these things before."

Then I felt bad. I liked seeing the bright colors on the items such as the placemats. I looked at them closely and imagined having them at home or giving them as gifts. I enjoyed the simple, colorfully painted desert scenes: a bright green cactus standing by a red hill with an orange sun in the background; a brown coyote howling off to the side—all these images well defined. I liked the bold designs on the rugs. I liked a lot that I saw. I felt belittled by Hannah for looking at these things, but then I realized something.

I turned to her. "Please don't feel sad," I told her. "I don't feel sad. When I pick up a placemat and look at items you think are cheap, it's not terrible. I can see them, so I like them. With my eyesight, it takes a lot of bright color and design for me to appreciate something. I want you to feel that I'm enjoying what I see. Just don't let me buy it if you think it's in bad taste."

That seemed to help. I promised to check with her before buying anything.

Hannah went to use a restroom and as I stood in an aisle waiting, with Teela beside me, a woman came out from in back of the store with a Golden Retriever puppy in her arms. She had seen Teela, who is half Golden Retriever and half Yellow Labrador, and had gone home to get her pup. As she held him up for me to see, I petted him; he was very soft. Teela rose on her back legs to smell him. I was glad to see the little dog close up, to see his head shaped like Teela's, as she must have been when she was a puppy. Suddenly I was back in a softer world, furry, full of something that gives to me, full of the life I take with me. I felt blessed by the generosity of a stranger, this woman who had brought me her pup. We bought no poncho and no placemats for my sister, but we did purchase a small golden wool rug with Mexican designs, made in India by the El Paso Saddle Blanket Company.

As we walked out of the log cabin trading post and I stepped into the fading daylight, the trucks pounded by on I-10. The empty parking lot outside the store seemed covered by a dirtier dust than back at Big Hatchet, which now felt very far away. I walked with Teela to a spot at the end of the lot so she could relieve herself and I looked up at the sky. In the west, a faint orange glow was accumulating and spreading overhead. Not bright orange as it had been in the early morning when I had stood in the lodge by the window and looked out at the deep rose color and then the fresh orange, an auspicious sign of the day to come. I had started the day with a sunrise that presaged good things, and now I was ending with a fainter orange sunset suggesting all I was leaving behind—spreading not over pine trees and wooded fields, nor over a magical barren landscape in front of a mountain, but here where a road returns.

This interstate was not my road; mine was a nearly invisible stretch of asphalt that could not be told apart from the desert plains around it. It led first through trees with bare branches that looked like golden filigree shimmering in the morning sun; then through a pass where I failed to see a mountain peak at the back of the Burro range; through Lordsburg, a town where it was hard to find an air pump and a tire gauge at the same time. A stop at Kranberry's where I saw paintings on walls outside restrooms; through white desert plains near phantomlike towns like Animas, where I had wished to stay. East through countryside I could barely see, so hazy was my vision in the sun. To Hachita with its boarded-up tavern, and Big Hatchet where I spent a long time trying to see a mountain in a desert basin.

My day had begun with optimism. All along, it was marked by my companionship with Hannah and Teela, and by my efforts both to see what was around me and to come to terms with my blindness.

We had a good dinner that night back up in Silver City and I slept well. Before I went to bed, I played with Teela on the floor of our room in the lodge. I was grateful for her and for Hannah and for my comfortable surroundings. But my dreams were back in that sunlit place where I had stood with my binoculars and looked up at a mountain and felt satisfied and happy. That moment was part of a longer day, a longer journey. I wanted to remember and hold close some lessons I had learned that day from my travels. Though I had tried to see with acuity the changing landscape around me, more important to me were my moments of acceptance—when I saw without binoculars or telephoto lens; when I relished the ghostlike, the fuzzy town, the cactus with invisible spikes, the smell of cooking grease, the excitement of being in a borderland, the fur of my guide dog, the love I felt from Hannah. I thought I'd let her take me back.

PART 2: LIGHTS IN THE DARK

Chapter 4

Crossing Borders

As we drove the thirty miles south from Deming, the sun glared and the land seemed inhospitable. Hannah and I had traveled east this morning from Silver City and were dipping south now into Mexico for lunch. The desert plains in all directions looked parched and brown. To the west, I saw three volcanic peaks sticking up abruptly from the flat land, the Tres Hermanas, or Three Sisters. I had hoped to see Big Hatchet in the distance, but either it was too far away or the Tres Hermanas blocked it. Earlier on our way, Hannah thought she saw Big Hatchet far off in the south shimmering almost invisibly in the sun. I took out my binoculars but failed to see it. Now I imagined it out in the vast plains, a glowing peak, so quickly a memory.

The road south of Deming felt rough, not in bad shape but I could feel its gritty hardness as we drove where nothing seemed remarkable. But just as I was wondering if this brief sojourn south would be worth it, the flat plains opened to reveal a town—some houses on side roads, a grain bin, a church, a gas station. This was Columbus, the last stop before the Mexican border. On its outskirts, we pulled off into a state park to get our bearings. I had heard of Pancho Villa State Park, named for the Mexican rebel and known for its cactus garden. While Hannah was looking at a map, I got out of the car and walked over to a grouping of tall,

51

arching cactus and yucca, then felt frustrated that I could not see them clearly. Their shapes seemed almost soft in the noon sunlight. Perhaps on the way back we could stop again and I could distinguish them better.

As we drove on, approaching the border, I began to notice dirt parking lots on the right of the road. Hannah started to pull off into one of them when I stopped her, thinking they were a last chance scheme to take our money. I asked her to drive over to the Border Patrol building across the street where I imagined there would be a fenced lot that would be safer. She did not think it necessary but drove across and pulled behind the building into a parking lot enclosed with barbed wire. A uniformed Border Patrol police officer came up to greet us immediately.

"You can't park here," he said. He then directed us back to the lots across the street. "It should be safe during the day," he added, then broke into a smile. He had noticed Teela in the backseat of the car. He began telling us about how when he was growing up in New Jersey, his brother had raised a guide dog. He liked the temperament of dogs like Teela. I felt surprised that on this border of Mexico, a man with a Hispanic accent was from New Jersey.

"You see," said Hannah as we drove back across the street, "sometimes you've got to trust me. I can see better than you can. I could tell this was where we should park."

I looked around at the half-empty parking lot as she spoke and I knew I had been afraid not only that some entrepreneurial men would take our money, but that when I got out of the car someone would try to steal Teela. And maybe the car would be looted when we left it. Hannah assured me this was where people parked. It would be safe. We locked the car, climbed from the sunken dirt lot to the sidewalk, and began walking. On the American side of the border, the sidewalk was clear and new. Where the road seemed to end, I followed Teela into a covered walkway, which felt dark and confusing, but in a few steps, it was light again. Suddenly I was in Mexico. When I looked down, the sidewalk appeared cracked, seemed old, and had chunks of cement sticking up. Many people milled around, mostly men and boys.

I grasped Teela's harness firmly as I walked behind Hannah. I prayed I would not trip, and that no one would reach out to take Teela or hurt my golden guide. The guide dog school had stressed that our dogs were very valuable. I watched out for Teela's well-being always. Now, in this unfamiliar place, I was all the more alert for danger. As I walked, I looked at the ground intently. I did not want to look up and see my surroundings, for fear I would seem unprotected. Instead, I focused straight ahead, walked purposefully. Cars came quickly and turned corners. One of the side streets was dirt. The curbs were high up, set at varying angles, some of them marked with red and highly visible, others gray and blended into the street. This view, a map of the surface of the ground, was my field of vision. I watched the surface carefully because I did not want to fall.

Walking the two blocks to reach the restaurant where we were headed felt to me like walking a gauntlet. I felt watched and uneasy. We had to cross several streets. Goods placed out on the sidewalks for sale stood in the way and I feared bumping into them. Hannah kept saying, "Follow me, it's all right. It's safe." "Cross now." "There are some men over there. They won't hurt you." But nothing relieved the apprehensiveness I felt, my sense of being on guard.

As we neared the restaurant, I saw a woman and a few boys sitting outside in front of the doorway. I heard one of the boys say "perro." I stiffened.

"That's just a child," Hannah told me. "He wants to know if he can pet the dog."

I had not expected to be so afraid. Inside the restaurant, my fear continued. I sat stock still at our table and looked around into a very busy darkness. The restaurant seemed large. I saw blurred shapes of wrought iron decorations, colored lights, displayed dishes, and statuary on the walls. Musicians with guitars and an accordion were playing music so loud it thundered through the room.

I asked Hannah to describe for me what she saw. "The musicians are behind you up on a little stage. I think they're at the end of their set. I hope they come back."

"What do you see on the walls?"

"Religious figures, candles, lots of lights and crosses, some flowers, a painting of a saint, I'm not sure which one."

"What do the people who are at the other tables look like?"

"Retired people. They're older."

"Older than us?"

"Yes. It looks like a group. I think they're about to leave. Someone should be taking our order soon."

I was aware of Teela at my feet. I did not want her licking the floor. I put my hands down to check her and to check my backpack, which I had rested against her to keep it off the floor. The floor was probably clean, but I wasn't taking chances. We waited a long time for our food. I did not eat much. I was eager to leave. But Hannah seemed content. The musicians made her happy. They finished and things quieted down, and oddly, I missed them.

On our way out of the restaurant, we stopped in at the adjoining store, stocked full with Mexican tourist items. This time, the ponchos were made from multicolored blankets; our friend would look like a Christmas tree; they were much too bright. Hannah searched and, in the rear of the store, found a more subdued blanket for our bed back at home, which I had been wishing for—it had earthen tones yet a bold design that I could see.

As we left, walking along the street back toward the border, Hannah carried the new blanket and I followed her, guided by Teela. Again, I feared the cracked sidewalks, the high curbs, the irregular street crossings. I could not tell, when I crossed a street, where the opposite sidewalk would be. I worried about bumping into the pottery displayed on the sidewalks for sale. I feared a hand would come out of the darkness at my sides and take Teela from me. I could not walk fast enough. It felt like a nightmare and I felt ashamed of my fears.

I had not been thinking about my blindness when we decided to go to Mexico. I had not thought about how much I have tunnel vision—that I see what is straight ahead and my eyes seem to move slowly, taking in new objects one at a time. Something coming from the darkness off to my side frightens me because it is invisible until it is directly in front of me. I see pieces of my surroundings, then work at grasping the whole.

I followed Hannah, who did not seem scared, as I was. She kept telling me what she saw: "Watch out for the planters on your left." "It's a big step up." "There are some men behind us, but don't worry." "Follow me. The sidewalk to your right has a long crack. I'm leading you around it."

Finally back on the American side of the border, I felt relieved. We checked through the Port of Entry and then drove north through the streets of Columbus, which seemed oddly clean and quiet compared with the streets half a mile away. I wanted to stop again at the park with the cactus garden. Hannah turned in at the gate and drove us farther back. In flat dirt expanses off the drive-through park road, huge cactus and succulents stood in circular plots next to wooden restrooms and near campsites. The plants looked as if they had been growing here for a long time. Some of the cactus, clustered together, reminded me of gnarled people with multiple arms reaching up, and I was a visitor in their midst. This was a strange garden, extensive, looped through by the road, the ancient plants so big they seemed to march across the lean space.

I got out of the car, leaving Teela and Hannah, and walked over to a hillside where giant gray-green agave plants, with clusters of uplifted swordlike staves, climbed toward a water tower in the sky. I stepped over to look closely at these agave and at nearby cactus, but I worried that I would get my eye poked if I bent close enough to see them, or I'd lose my balance and fall into a sharp plant. I took out my camera and then my binoculars, trying to see more clearly the triangular edges of the agave, the spines of the barrel cactus, the branches of the tall mesquite. Yet my vision was murky even with these aids. I could not get the edges defined. The sun was low in the sky now, shining through the golden spines of the cactus, creating a halo around each one, and shining through the shimmering green agave as, like small soldiers, they ascended the hill. I viewed them with my naked eye for a sense of the landscape and marveled at these majestic plants, at this garden on a grand scale—an odd kind of preserve in a very flat place, crossed by a winding road, the cactus standing pristinely like statuary on dusty ground a stone's throw, it felt, from the parking lot next to the border.

It was so different here. Not crowded, no people, just giant plants, space, and quiet. It was a peaceful retreat for me, a reminder of what I liked, even though I could not see it well. It wasn't confusing for me to be among these old plants. I thought it magical, and I was glad for it, though I was still feeling upset by my lack of sight, by my sense of Hannah's dwindling patience, by the fear I had experienced when across the border, a fear I had not expected.

My anxieties were stressful for all three of us. Hannah felt responsible for me, and I for Teela, whom I knew could feel my concerns at the other end of her leather harness. My previous view of a border town did not include how vulnerable I would feel there. And while some of my response was to the poverty in Mexico, much of it was because of my eyesight. When planning this trip, I had not taken into account that when I stepped across that geographic border, I would also step across a visual border and into a confusing space, becoming frightened to the point of terror. Most of the time back at home, I take for granted my tunnel vision, the darkness around me, the fact that I miss pieces of the visual world. When something hits me in the face and I do not see it coming, or when I suddenly feel myself falling, I do become afraid. But I enjoy a basic level of security in familiar surroundings where sidewalks have similar heights and stepping down from one leads to another. Chaos when blind is hard.

They had not prepared us in guide dog school for dealing with situations where you feel your dog might be stolen. Before this trip, I had been mostly worried about Teela getting worms, not about hands reaching out from invisible sides of the street taking her away. To take Teela from me is to remove my sense of safety, of being given to, of moving with confidence and pride despite my lack of sight. When I was making motel reservations a few months earlier, I told a motel clerk I was traveling with a guide dog, and she had surprised me when she said, "Of course it's fine to bring her. She's your eyes." I felt reassured by this recognition of my need. I think of Teela most often as simply a dog when she is, in fact, also a guide. I think of myself as sighted even when I am blind.

That lunch in Mexico made me feel ashamed for feeling so scared when across the border, and it made me aware of how much I fear what I don't see. It made me conscious of my needs for order and for reassurance about my safety. They say that a blind person does well with a lot of organization. One reason I do well with not seeing is that I tend to be very organized; I like having things in their place and paying attention to detail.

As we drove out of the ancient cactus garden and headed north, I felt unsettled, glad for the images of the cactus and agave replacing my images of the cracked streets of Mexico, but I was still churning inside in a kind of inner dark space. Behind me stretching out in the fading sunlight, slipping farther and farther away, was a juxtaposition of near opposites that I wanted not to be so: dark and light, rich and poor, sighted and blind.

TRUTH OR CONSEQUENCES

We continued north on a route that would eventually lead us to the Rio Grande. We stopped for gas. At the station, I stood and looked into the distance beyond dry fields, trying to understand what I could not see, feeling Hannah was worried because we had miles yet to travel and were far from food and rest. Then in

Deming, we stopped at a bookstore, where I searched for something about Big Hatchet, perhaps a picture of the mountain, some more information, a map. I found nothing. We drove on, turned east. The sun was now very low in the sky, softening the appearance of the surrounding landscape. The feeling was open and endless. The road stretched into emptiness, desert surrounding us. Then in the midst of plains the color of winter wheat shining gently in the setting sun, we stopped at a sign that read, "Middle of Nowhere Bar and Cafe." I had stopped at this spot on trips before, simply to stand under the sign and marvel at the yellow grasslands and the sense of isolation. On a hill overlooking the road and the sign stood a trailer, which I assumed contained the bar and grill, but I never took it seriously. For me, the sign was enough.

The last time Hannah and I passed this way, the sun had been setting, too, and afterward, the sky had turned bright orange—completely, in all directions, ever deepening, lasting until a full moon rose beyond the mountains in the east and the sky there turned a dark ink blue. My eyesight had already begun to fade at that time and the bright orange all around me lifted my spirits, as did the white circle of the moon clearly visible against the surrounding darkness. Although I could not see details, I could take joy in the drama of those large blocks of color and light. This evening, however, there was no color in the sky and I saw less well than I had just a year ago.

We parked beneath the Middle of Nowhere sign. Feeling hopeful, I got out of the car so I could look up at the sky without the interference of the tinted car windows. I saw a faint pink color touch clouds over a mountain to the north. The small patch of color glowed through only a few of the gray clouds. As I watched it, I began to mourn my lack of sight. I regretted that the heavens did not stage a colorful light show just when I wanted it. I was out of sorts. I was tired. We had really tried. But it's hard traveling in strange places without seeing well; it's hard going around wanting miracles, special experiences, things to remember and savor, and instead feeling ashamed at a border, seeing cactus that look blurred and sunsets that appear faded.

As we drove east in the dusk, I began thinking about where we were headed next, toward a treat for Hannah. I had reserved a room in a lodge where she could soak in a hot tub and get a massage the next day. We could have dinner there if we got in late and Hannah did not want to drive farther. I wanted this special place to reward her for all her driving and good spirits and willingness to take me places, and because she has back troubles, and because I love her.

We wound our way through the chile fields of Hatch and up the Rio Grande. It was dark as we neared the spreading lights of Truth or Consequences. Hannah seemed happy, though I think we were both anxious. We drove into the center of the town, then pulled over to the side of a dark street walled by the black windows of closed stores. Christmas lights hung from lampposts overhead quietly decorating the night. Hannah took out a map and looked at it under the ceiling light of the car. Only one main street looped through downtown Truth or Consequences, but here it divided before it came back together. I had been through this town many times before—stopping for groceries, gas, or a place to eat. Even in the dark, I thought I could direct us to where we would be staying.

"We turn left up ahead," I said to Hannah.

"You always think you know," she answered worriedly. "I don't want to get lost." She looked again at the map, which I felt could not be as precise as my memories.

She drove us left, then right, then back left again. The deserted dark streets felt oddly wide for a small town. One block from the main street, the space opened out into a still darkness. Then up ahead, a wall lined with electric luminarias surrounded inner Christmas lights on the facade of a building I could not see except for a sense of its being lit up and large, with recessed archways. We turned in on a gravel drive and parked.

Stepping out of the car, I followed Hannah along a paved pathway uphill to the front of the building as Teela pulled me forward excitedly. Near the entrance, the cement path turned into a red carpet. Lights shining through the glass doors ahead glowed in the dark. I was startled. This seemed like a hotel. I suddenly wanted to flee, to go back to the cactus garden, the open desert, the western lodge where we had spent the night before, to a cabin off in the woods somewhere.

I stepped into the bright lobby, walked past couches on my right, a Christmas tree next to a piano on my left. I had not expected this degree of formality or that here in a town named for a quiz show—whose main feature was a water tower on a hill above downtown and the underlying hot springs that ran beneath the ground, and a history of funky old bathhouses—there would be a hotel with a red carpet. A woman at the front desk wore a very proper green dress. Behind her, a brightly lit staircase, also covered with red carpet, ascended to the next floor. Above the staircase hung a glistening glass chandelier. I stepped up to a polished wooden counter and asked about our room.

The receptionist quite cordially checked on it, searched in her desk, and found some keys.

"Follow me," she said, coming out from behind the counter and leading us up the carpeted staircase, where I probed the ground with my toe to determine my footing. The steps were narrow and high, the red carpeting cushy; I worried about how I would do carrying our luggage or simply walking up and down these stairs with Teela. It felt odd—plush red carpeting and a big dog.

Upstairs, the receptionist led me down a hallway and opened the door to a room filled with a bed, a standing wood closet, and a tub next to a glass doorway draped with a red velvet curtain. Outside was a small balcony. "It's for cooling off after soaking," the receptionist said. I felt claustrophobic and frightened. Where were my open plains? Where were the small houses low to the ground where I like to stay? How did I manage to get us booked into the upstairs of a hotel? But this establishment was not called a hotel. It was called "The Sierra Springs Lodge and Spa."

The receptionist, named Sally, explained how this lodge used to be an apartment building, but it was completely redone. It had only been open for two years. "It was a boarding house before the conversion," she told us.

I asked to see another room.

"They're all the same. This is one of the nicer rooms," she added. "There's a man next door. But he's already taken his soak. He won't be using the balcony tonight. It's all yours."

Hannah was ready to bring up our bags. She had put her shoulder pack down on the bed.

"Is there another stairway?" I asked, hoping there would be another way to take Teela out, one easier for me to go up and down than the main front carpeted stairway.

"Of course," Sally said. "There's a back staircase that will take you out closer to the parking area."

I followed her down the hall where she opened a side door and I stepped out onto a cement landing. Despite a light above the doorway, the stairway below was dark. I could see nothing. The long staircase had no banister. I was shocked and afraid. I would not be able to use it. And although the staircase was at fault, I immediately felt that I was not brave enough, not skilled enough. I wished I had mastered walking up and down stairs without seeing, that I had perfected my balance in the dark. I felt incomplete as a blind person, not adequately competent, and ready to cry. I thought about calling ahead to the inn where we would spend the next night to ask if we could come early.

Hannah looked at the staircase. "Isn't there another room?" she asked Sally. "Do you have something downstairs?"

"The casita?" I interjected. I had read in the lodge materials that there was a small casita unit on the grounds with its own hot tub, but you had to stay there for two nights and it was expensive.

Sally seemed puzzled. "I'll check," she said and led us back down the hall to the main stairway. I glanced in at our room as we passed. It had a western feel, spare, though not inelegant. Still, I couldn't leave it quickly enough. I wanted to get back down to a floor on the ground, as if it were me and not Teela who might have to pee in the night and need to be rushed out.

At the front desk, I waited with Hannah while Sally consulted on the phone with someone. "I can show you the casita if you'd like," she said. "And we have another room on this floor. John is checking on it. Would you like me to give you a tour of the grounds while you wait?"

"Very much," I said.

She took a set of keys and led us out the front door of the lodge, then turned left. In a few steps more, there was darkness and cool air. Hannah followed Sally, I followed Teela following them. "If you see any steps, let me know," I called to Hannah, for I knew I would not see them in the dark and I worried that Teela might not stop me in time. Sally graciously led us along the front side of the broad lodge building, pointing things out as we passed them. A few paces ahead, she stopped and gestured to her left. "There's a gravel area over there, where your dog can go," she said. I reached down and picked up some pieces of the gravel, which felt sharp to me. I was afraid for Teela's paws. In a few more steps, Sally stopped again and pointed to a spot on the ground. "This is a hot tub." I couldn't quite grasp it. "It has a cover on it," Hannah whispered to me. The invisible tub was completely sunken beneath the ground and covered with a round piece of dark wood that looked much like the surrounding flagstone. I bent down to touch the cover to make it feel real, as I was increasingly learning to do with things I could not see, replacing my eyesight with my sense of touch.

"We can fill this tub for you if you like; it's empty now," Sally offered. "But you might prefer the spa." With that, she stepped back toward the large building behind us and opened a glass double door onto a room that glowed iridescent green and felt steamy and suggestive of places I had never been, of jungles and the undersea. From within the glowing room, a shiny metal railing emerged from a large sunken pool lit gently with green lights and smelling of perfume.

"Hannah, you might like that," I said. As in my mind, I saw another tub—the hot tub near the casita farther out in back of the lodge that I had seen in pictures with my magnifier. It was outdoors and had a rounded shape. I had thought Hannah and I might sit in that tub in privacy looking up at the stars, warm on a cold night, bathing, a kind of dessert for our day.

Sally stood waiting. "We can fill the spa for you. We fill it fresh for each guest. You are our only guests tonight who'll be using it. Just let me know."

As she closed the glass doors to the green spa, I felt relieved to be outdoors again. I stepped into the darkness and, led by Teela, followed Sally and Hannah around toward the back of the lodge. Soon the ground changed beneath my feet—from cement to flagstone, to gravel, and back again to flagstone. There were crevices and small steps up where I feared tripping. I did not fully trust Teela to stop and warn me about the small cracks and ridges. Teela is a fast-paced dog. She strides straight ahead day or night. Even at guide dog school, I'd had trouble at night. I had frozen when she tried to walk fast in the total darkness. A brisk walk and a missed step and there I would be, flat on my face, Teela having charged forward in search of a distant doorway or a curb at the next street. The grounds in back of The Sierra Springs Lodge weren't the split sidewalks of Mexico; they were landscaped flagstone and rock, but they had similar irregularities, no straight edges, many places for my toes to catch.

Hannah, sensing my fear, offered me her arm. I took it, linked it firmly through mine on my right, held Teela's harness with my left hand, and lurched forward. I was trying to keep Teela from speeding so I could stay attached to Hannah. I felt foolish but safely upright. The surroundings were very dark. This was a night without a moon. "Even I can't see much," Hannah said as we jagged along.

"There's a light somewhere here," Sally called and walked off in search of it.

I sensed a low building nearby, some prickly landscaping plants, flagstone at my feet. I stepped forward and walked into a wide cement cylinder shoulder high sticking up from the ground. The cement felt rough. This was not my idea of a romantic hot tub out in front of the casita, but that's what it was. A wooden ladder stood up against the tub's tall rounded outer wall. To enter, you climbed up the ladder to the top of the wall and lowered yourself in.

"It's too cold," Hannah shuddered.

"Where were my stars?" I wondered. I looked up into a black sky. Were there no stars up there, or could I not see them? The sides of the cement hot tub would be too high for me to manage with comfort. "Okay," I said to Hannah. "We won't soak here."

Linked once more to her and Teela, I stepped forward carefully and up a small step that no one seemed to tell me about. We were at the front door of the low casita now. Sally pushed open the door, turned on inner lights, and there was a little home—a living room with a stone fireplace, a wood floor with a woven center rug, a bedroom with a bed and soft lights and the same tub unit as in the room upstairs.

"We'll take it," I said.

"There's more." Sally led us through the rest of the casita, which had a separate wing with a kitchen, a guest room, a computer in the dining room. Back in the first bedroom, Hannah noticed coins on the dresser, and in the living room, papers scattered on a table.

"Someone's living here," she said.

"The owner stays here when he's in town," Sally explained. "Though he's not here now. He's in France."

"We'd only use half the space," I offered.

As we walked back to the lodge, I felt more relaxed, but I was confused by having been so afraid about my footing earlier, so untrusting of my dog. What good was a guide dog if I wouldn't dare follow her? At the time, I did not think that it would take a while for me to learn to trust Teela in the dark, that perhaps no one trusted their dog entirely at first.

At guide dog school, those of us with some vision could be reassured by our sight; trust would come more slowly to us perhaps. Those students with total blindness or near total blindness had to trust their dogs sooner. In those months after I left the guide dog school, it was amazing to me how often my thoughts turned back to it, as if all of life's lessons were to be found in that one month's experience, all my guides for how to be when blind, all my guides for how to be.

Back in the lodge lobby, I waited with Hannah for John, who would tell us about using the casita. Soon he appeared, a friendly, black-haired man wearing a white shirt and black pants. The price for the casita, however, was too steep.

"I have a room on this floor you might like instead," John offered. "It's quiet. It's down the hall behind the restaurant. Would you like to see it?"

"Yes."

"The room is odd, you'll see. It shares heat with the restaurant, but I can move in a small heater in case you get cold later."

He led us down a long tiled hallway past utility rooms, toward the kitchen. Someone trundled by with a metal table on wheels and smiled, I think, perhaps seeing Teela. John stepped forward and opened the door to a room on my right with a tan tiled floor, a bed with a white spread, white walls, a tub in the corner, two windows with white curtains. The room seemed plain and appealing.

"I can get a TV in here for you, if you'd like," John said. "I promise you, it'll be quiet. The restaurant closes in an hour. We don't open until 11 tomorrow. You'll be the only ones here. Right now, we don't have the key; but we'll find one."

"I can bring you robes and slippers for the spa," Sally offered. She had followed us in.

"Why didn't they show us this room first?" Hannah asked me when the two of us were next alone.

I began mumbling about how I had wanted to see the casita when John returned minutes later to try out a key. Then he took me out to show me a side door several steps down the hall.

"This is our delivery entrance, but no one's going to be using it tonight," he said. "Some cars are parked out there now, but they'll be gone soon. You can take your dog out here. I'll leave the door propped open for you overnight so it won't lock."

I was amazed. Such courtesy, so many efforts to take care of me. I was also frightened by the darkness outside when he opened the back door. There were three steps down on a small concrete staircase, but there was no railing. In the dark, I could not see the stairs or the cars that were supposedly parked outside that would be leaving later. I stepped cautiously down the steps, then bent and scooped up some gravel from the ground. It was sharp again. I didn't want to go out there in the night, but I smiled at John.

"Thank you very much," I said. "I really appreciate it."

Hannah and I returned to the room to decide. "I like it here," I said.

"It's the disabled room," Hannah noted as she looked around. "There are grab bars on the tub."

"Oh," I said, wondering if the room ever had been used before, and why it was so hidden. And wondering, too, why I had never thought of asking for a disabled room. I had a dog. But she wasn't disabled. Nor, in my mind, was I. I simply could not see well. But I could climb stairs. I could lift things. Next time, maybe I would ask for a disabled room so they wouldn't put me upstairs.

I went out to the car to start bringing in our bags and to take Teela to relieve herself where I thought she would be happy—on cement and flat dirt near the car. Sally came with me to help me with the bags. It was beginning to feel not entirely odd now—my walking out the front door of a lit-up lodge with arching windows and a red carpeted entryway, walking down in the darkness on a curved cement path, lights shining at my feet, going to the car, carrying up my suitcase, Teela in tow following me, her leash attached to my belt.

I was beginning to feel less afraid. We took the room. When I brought in our last bags, a television set with two cookies wrapped in a cloth napkin on top of it stood at the foot of the bed.

"Will you be having dinner?" John asked, stopping by.

"Yes," Hannah said.

We got ready quickly. I fed Teela in the bathroom, suitable for a wheelchair, now occupied by a dog, and stepped out with her and with Hannah. We walked down to the lobby. At the main entrance to the restaurant, behind a front counter, John was standing with Sally and with half a dozen other people who looked to me like staff, though they were blurry in my view. "We're here for dinner," Hannah announced to a hushed attentiveness. A hostess in black led us to a table. The restaurant was empty, softly lit, a long narrow room with cloth-covered small tables and brightly colored glassware on a mantle. I glanced quickly at my surroundings as Teela guided me by the tables.

"Did you notice?" Hannah whispered after we sat down, "all the people at the desk?"

"Was it because I made a fuss about the room?"

"They were looking at the dog," she said. "They were smiling."

I had seen the people but not the smiles. I had been focusing on Teela's back, on maneuvering in a small space and not seeming too conspicuous.

I smiled now, glad to be greeted with friendliness.

We had unusual service in the restaurant that night. The only other group sat at the farther end of the long room. One then another waitress came over to offer us bread, then wine, then our meal, and I felt they were visiting, checking us out—these two odd women with a guide dog. The food was delicious and generous, more upscale than I would normally feel comfortable with, but I was grateful for it. John, apparently, was the chef. He came out to ask how we had liked our meal. We thanked him and everybody for our dinner. When we walked back to our room, we stopped at the lodge check-in desk. Earlier, I had asked Hannah, "Would you like to use the spa tonight?"

"It's late," she had said. "And you don't like that kind of thing. I can go by myself in the morning."

At the desk now, I told Sally we would like to take a soak. She would fill the spa pool for us. It would take about forty minutes.

Back in our room while we waited, I lay on the bed with the white spread and looked up at the ceiling. This was certainly an adventure. Hannah began to unpack. Teela took her place on the floor beside me. John had brought in a small heater, which now stood near the foot of the bed. I felt in such a different world than I had earlier in the day at lunchtime in Mexico. It was hard for me to believe that my experience across the border and this at the lodge were part of the same day. Yet my fears, my needs for reassurance, and the centrality of my vision had a continuity. After the allotted time, I got up and put on the white terrycloth robe and slippers that Sally had laid out, and taking a towel, I walked with Hannah and Teela toward the lobby of the lodge. We stepped through the big room, heading for the side door and the spa. Never before had I walked through a hotel lobby wearing only a robe. Sally had said it was fine, but it must have looked unusual—two lesbians carrying towels, dressed in white robes, slippering bashfully toward the outdoors, one led by a large golden dog.

I followed Teela, who followed Hannah. Sally trailed after us. "Would you like cold drinks for the spa?" she asked us at the door to the warm room. After letting us inside, she left and soon returned with a pitcher of lemonade and ice and two large plastic glasses.

"Are the glasses dark green or blue?" I asked Hannah not

long after, wanting to know the color, the detail, and how they fit in with my surroundings, as if I could not bear to have this information missing.

"Maybe a bluish green," Hannah said, closing the glass double doors to the spa so we would have privacy. I stepped down into the warm water of the large pool. The room looked even more iridescent green this time. The square pool was light green. The ceiling was green; the walls had light green murals painted on them. In two far corners of the room, white Grecian pillars stood with nothing on top of them. A gentle, pungent scent spread through the room, a mixture of herbs and flowers, cucumbers, roses, eucalyptus. Beside the pool, near the glass doors, was a wooden bench. I no longer felt afraid of the spa, as I had earlier. I tied Teela's leash to the shiny metal railing that led down into the water, putting her far enough away so I hoped she would not try to get in and swim, but near enough so that she could feel with us.

Then I stepped back into the inviting water, which felt so warm. The entire space around me, bathed in soft green light, appeared blurred so that the pretentious pillars and the content of the scenes painted on the walls did not disturb me. The steam from the hot water moistened the room and made it dreamlike. The herbal scent freshened the air. Hannah turned off the lights overhead and lit the space with candles. In this warm, enveloping, naturally fuzzy world, my eyesight felt at home. I did not have to focus on anything but Hannah's naked body reflecting the candlelight. I focused on the water lit from below, on getting in and out of the pool, on the marvel of my being here. Invigorated, I swam over to Hannah and dipped under her, arose holding her, tracing the outline of her body with my fingers, feeling the minerals softening her skin. She held and stroked me. Teela cried from her perch beside the pool and stood up, wanting to be part of us.

"It's okay, girl. Down." She settled.

The light flickered in the green water illuminated from below. "Look," Hannah said, pointing to the bottom of the pool. "Fish are down there." I looked, trying to see them, but I couldn't. I'd have to take her word for it. Something was painted on the bottom of the tub. I was content having it blurry.

Hannah turned on the overhead lights for a moment. I opened the glass doors to let in cooler air from outside. Steam rose in a rush and filled the room.

"Get back down in the pool," Hannah said. "People will see you." But no one was out in the empty parking lot in the dark night.

Back in the pool, I floated with Hannah. She held me as I lay on my back in the water. We glided together, then apart, then back together, delighting in each other, caressing, touching, moving breast to breast. When I got too warm, I sat on the wooden bench next to Hannah. We sipped our drinks, murmuring about our good fortune. Hannah took out a foam mat, spread it on the bench, lay down, and I rubbed her back where it tended to get sore.

She joined me again in the tub where we floated with the candles throwing flickering illuminations on the walls and in the water. I was strangely unafraid. Hannah held me gently. We kissed. We swirled together and apart, glad for the moment, knowing each other so well, circling back and forth through the warm water, moving sweetly as in a dance. We embraced.

"Teela, it's okay. Down."

"I love you," Hannah said.

"I love you, too."

"You brought us here," she added thoughtfully.

"You didn't think I'd come in this tub with you, did you?" I kidded her.

It felt joyful. I was pleased to be so happy. So much of my day had been spent with worrying and fears and planning things so they would work out all right, struggling with views of myself that find me lacking. I had not been able to drive, but I could get us here.

"I'm content," Hannah said. "I can leave whenever you want."

"One more time," I asked, and she joined me in the water and we floated and held each other, and I laughed and laughed.

"You're overtired," Hannah whispered.

Very reluctantly, an hour and a half after we had come to the pool, we left that feeling of comforting warmth and fuzziness and protected closeness. We donned the white robes and walked back through the lobby to our disabled room. That night, I lay in bed tired, fed, satisfied, feeling something special had happened. I lay next to Hannah and thought back on the day. So many fears, so many new places. I had not had time to process it. I knew only that people had made a difference, that much as I was affected strongly by places—by my physical surroundings—I could not wander all alone. What other people did mattered—Hannah, the lodge staff. I needed comfort and safety, counterposed to the dangers of the cracked sidewalks, the dark stairs, the jagged flagstone and sharp gravel. I had liked the cactus I saw that afternoon with their spikes, the agave with their sharp edges; I liked knowing they were out there. But at night I needed an inner space that was soft and reassuring. I could spend my life looking for the edges of things, and for irregularities in the ground where I might trip. I could spend my time feeling for these borders, and worrying about them, but I needed not to. I needed to get inside my experiences and think about them, to get outside them and portray them in order to see them.

I was so often a failure in my own eyes. I could not drive. I could not see well. I got scared of new countries and strange rooms. I became irritable when I had to follow Hannah when I feared I could not trust her. I kept wanting to leave where I was and get somewhere else. I did not like being a spectacle, having people look at me all the time because I had a guide dog, though with my lack of vision, fortunately, I often did not notice. I was happy to be in the desert, but I still struggled with ambivalence about my acceptability. My blindness made me feel both more and less acceptable than previously. Because of it, people did extra things for me, but I did not want them to resent me for it.

I find traveling in strange places to be daunting; always there's the threat of coldness, of an inhospitable world. My blindness softens things, however. It makes the world more friendly, more interesting, and more peculiar; it makes my environment feel less foreign at the same time as it is more foreign and only partially visible.

Because of my lack of eyesight, I focus more on what I do see. I want to notice everything. And in a way, what I see is simpler than if I had better vision. I do not judge it as much. I take joy in it, except when it frightens me. Every look, every turn is some sort of picture for me, surprising and to be relished because it is there.

I smiled now as I lay with Hannah in the tan-tiled room with the white walls and white spread. We'd made it. We had gone south and come back. Most of all, we had done it together and we were happy with each other. We were having magical experiences. We were holding each other close. I had Teela. She was safe, tied to the bed near me with her leash, sleeping now on her blanket, glad for her rest. "Thank you. Good guide, girl," I reached down and patted her head. I had begun a ritual of thanking Teela each night for guiding me that day.

I closed my eyes and lay back. "Goodnight sweetheart," I said to Hannah.

"I love you," she murmured from the depths of her pillow.

"I'll leave the key on top of the television when I go out in the morning."

I was looking forward to breakfast, to strong coffee, to an early walk in the town while Hannah slept and then had a massage. I had my dog. I could go places.

Chapter 5

Morning Walk

The next morning while Hannah slept, I started out early to explore the streets near the lodge. As I stepped outside and walked down the path toward the front gate, I looked back up at the adobe colored building glowing a golden tan in the morning sun. The lodge looked far warmer in the early morning than it had at night, far less harsh and intimidating, a lone Spanish-style building on a hill, the sun shining on its face. I stepped outside the gate, guided by Teela, then peered in both directions on the quiet street ahead. I thought I would go to the right; it seemed to lead to open spaces where I could walk. But I soon ran out of sidewalk when I reached a main road cutting into this smaller one. I did not want to get hit by a car that I would not see coming fast downhill, and the area looked rather barren, so I turned around and walked back to the lodge gate to start again.

From there, setting out in the opposite direction, I knew I would have to keep careful track of my steps, actually my crossings—the number of streets I crossed, when I made turns, and on which side of the street I was when I took a turn. I needed to do this in order to trace my way back later, for I could not make out the lettering on the street signs. This area of town was full of streets unfamiliar to me. I did not want to get lost and have to call the lodge for directions. I walked to the corner of the sunny street on which the lodge seemed to be at the farther end; I turned right and crossed the street, then walked down a block and crossed a second small street. Near the next corner, I began passing a low square building, where I noticed a large green agave plant sitting in front. The plant with its artichoke shape and upraised pointed staves reassured me. The low building beside it stood next to a wide commercial street and had a bold sign saying it was a bank. I thought I would remember the agave and the low bank as a way to know when I should turn right off the main street on my return.

Cautiously, I crossed the wide commercial street, heading toward what looked like interesting stores on the other side. I turned right and walked up to a closed pharmacy, then turned back and continued along a side street until my interest in houses and yards there petered out, for they looked plain and blurred. I came back to the corner. Nothing distinct was planted on it to help me identify it on my return. From this side of the commercial street, it was hard for me to distinguish the bank and the agave across the way since I had to be up close to things to see them with definition. I needed to get my bearings and wondered how I should proceed. Should I cross back to the side of the street with the bank, or continue to my right on this farther side, where I was afraid I might get lost?

I was struggling to remember the count of streets I had already passed: I had started at the lodge front gate, then I had turned left for a long block, or was it two? Or a long block cut by a driveway? I had turned right, crossed a side street, then crossed another street, then reached the corner with the bank and the agave next to the commercial street. I had crossed that street, seen a closed pharmacy to my right, not turned right but walked straight ahead until the potentially interesting stores petered out into hazy-looking yards and houses. I had walked back to the corner across from the bank and was now considering turning right. But I had to remember that a right turn for me here would be a left turn if I looked at it in terms of what would have happened if I had not taken my detour up the side street and back.

I wanted, at that moment, to write my directions down on a piece of paper. But my paper was buried deep in my bag, and I thought that if I wrote down my turns and crossings, I would be constantly stopping and taking off my gloves, and I worried that I would not be able to read my handwriting—even my writing in large black letters on white paper looks blurred to me. I'd have to take out my magnifier to read it letter by letter, and it hardly seemed worth it. I preferred to try to remember, to learn new skills for finding my way. I could see physical landmarks to some extent—the streets, the storefronts, large plants—but not with enough precision. I would have to rely on nonvisual clues as well. I thought back on my route thus far and turned right, staying on the pharmacy side of the street and following Teela, who had been dutifully patient during my travels up and down the side streets. Trained as a guide dog, she could lead me around obstacles and stop at curbs, but I had to tell her exactly where I wanted to go, both in setting out and later on our return. A bloodhound might follow a scent back, but Teela relied on me to remember our route. Left to her own devices, I knew, she might happily decide to do some exploring of her own, and I would become even more lost.

"Right," I instructed my eager companion and we turned. As we walked past stores not yet open, I looked carefully into the windows, hoping to decipher the nature of each business. It felt like a game, trying to figure out the stores. Teela stopped with me promptly at each window, started again, walked to the next storefront and peered in with me—at a bar, closed, but with the floors being washed out, smelling of disinfectant; we passed a gift shop with some lacy material in the window, a boarded-up building, a narrow dark space, then a window with books, a bookstore. I followed Teela to the recessed entryway, opened the door and stepped inside.

Here I felt at home. Although I could no longer read the print in books, they were my element. After all, I was writing one. Two people, a man and a woman, were bustling around, getting the store ready for the morning. I thought perhaps there would be a cup of coffee waiting for me on a table in back and I'd find a book about Big Hatchet and sip the coffee and, if not read the book, then look forward to its contents. But the store was fairly dark and I smelled no coffee. I asked the man if they had any books about Big Hatchet. He seemed not to recognize it. "It's south of Hachita," I said. "It's a mountain."

"Our books about wilderness are in back," he said, not looking up from what he was doing.

"Where exactly in back?" I asked, thinking this might clue him in to the fact that I needed more than a general direction, because I could not see.

He lifted his head and gestured with it toward his right shoulder.

I shook my head in response. "I can't tell where you mean. Can you take me there?"

He reluctantly led me to a room in the back of the store, where on a high shelf was the section he had mentioned. Pointing toward it, he left me and walked back up front. I looked around. There was no way in this dimly lit store that I was going to be able to read the titles on used books, for I was beginning to realize this was a used bookstore. I quickly considered my options. I could take out my lighted magnifier and shine it on the dark spines of the books, but I would then have to open them and pore through their musty pages to find out if there was any reference to Big Hatchet. Then I'd need to locate the page referred to, with my magnifier, and read a bit of it to see if it was worth reading further, enough so that I should buy the book. Or I could come back later with Hannah and have her help me.

I turned and walked back to the middle room of the store and got the clerk who had left me. "I can't see well," I said, ignoring, as he had, the signifying presence of my dog. "Could you look with me and tell me if any of those books would have information about Big Hatchet?"

Miffed, he came back and quickly glanced at the shelf. "We don't have any," he said.

I left.

My experiences are not often like that. I do not usually get abandoned and spoken to disdainfully when I ask for simple help, so it reminded me of what can happen. But the important thing for me was that I had determined that there was no hidden find. Though I had wanted the information, that there was nothing in the store about Big Hatchet affirmed my feelings about the mystery of the mountain and the magic of its looming presence.

As Teela and I walked farther down the street, I began to think that the interesting stores were now on the other side. Yet the commercial street I would have to cross to reach them seemed wider here than it had earlier, perhaps because there was more traffic on it, for the 9 a.m. hour had passed. The stores on both sides of the street were becoming more dense, as I was entering the busier part of the small downtown. I wanted to cross the main street, but the traffic was coming fast, and I was worried that I would lose my bearings. How many side streets had I already crossed? Could I retrace my steps back to the lodge? I had no sense of north, south, east, or west. I was simply going left and right. It might have helped if I had a sense of compass directions, but I had always before found my way around places by feel and by my sight. I had a better visual memory than I did a memory for counting streets.

I decided to walk back to the corner where I had started out, across from the pharmacy and diagonally across the main street from the bank. I walked purposefully. Once there, I took a deep breath, told Teela to go forward, crossed the street quickly, and stepped up the high curb on the other side.

I turned right and started out again in the direction from which I had come, heading away from the low bank and toward the downtown. I passed some nondescript empty stores, then offices, a closed restaurant, a down curb, a crossing, an up curb, then a beauty shop, a used clothing store, knickknacks in a window, a down curb, a side street, then up a disabled ramp, some more stores. Everything felt brownish to me, as if the sidewalks were made of wood, though they were not. At each storefront, I tried to determine what kind of store it was. Only a few had their names close enough for me to see, at eye level in a window, on a door, or on a low-hanging sign. As I walked on, the storefronts became more interesting and more cluttered, as if there was more in each for sale, and quite a few were open. Sometimes, a store had two doors and when I stepped up to one, it was locked and I had to go to the other. I did not want to stop too frequently at the doors, for this would be hard for Teela. They told us at guide dog school that if we stopped too often when searching for a store, our dogs would get confused and feel that was how to walk down a street—you went up to every door, then back out again as a way of traveling forward rather than following a more direct route.

Several times when I was not certain about a store but wanted to know, I opened the front door and popped my head in. "What kind of store is this?" I asked. "Thank you," I then said upon leaving, feeling that I had to walk through the store a bit first, that I owed the owner or the person who had told me about the store a cursory once over. "Nice store," I'd say after having made my way around aisles full of wool for knitting or racks of winter jackets.

I entered one store that sold tourist items—little sculptures, pottery, rugs, tiles, pictures with colorful scenes. I searched in the postcard racks for a photo of Big Hatchet. It was amazing to me how many other things looked like the mountain. Then on close inspection with my magnifier, what I thought was the dome and peak turned out to be a roadrunner, Elephant Butte, or a picture of a flower. In the book racks, I surveyed the larger titles, but there were too many titles I might overlook. I thought I'd bring Hannah back with me later. I walked on and reached a restaurant that I had stopped at on one of our trips before. Maybe we could come here for lunch. A little farther, I decided to turn around.

Walking back now, I stopped and stood at the edge of the

main street and looked across to the other side. There was a museum over there that I might go into and an open space that looked like a parking lot, where Teela and I could sit in the sun. I wanted to explore the other side of the street, though the cars were coming quickly. I stepped down off the sidewalk, told Teela to go forward, looked both ways, began to cross, then immediately stepped back—deciding I had better not brave it. I continued on, somewhat sad because I hadn't walked for as long as I wanted or explored further. I had an image of myself—as I used to be—before my vision loss, simply setting out, walking everywhere, exploring side streets indefatigably, with no limits. And fantasy though it was, I felt a pang of regret that I was no longer so mobile. Then I looked down at Teela's broad back and golden fur, reminding myself that she was my comfort now, my new adventure. I might be more limited because of my blindness, but walking with her, I felt an intangible freedom.

As we headed back briskly along the main thoroughfare, I stepped down a curb and across a side street almost before I knew it was there. How many of these small crossings did I not register on my way over, so interested had I been in deciphering the window displays? We passed beyond the more cluttered storefronts, and then something about the way the street curved or divided confused me. My walk back was beginning to feel like a blur—a dusty, windy, sun-speckled blur. I was walking quickly, following Teela. Finally, I saw the low bank, although not at first the agave. I had to pass the corner and turn right to find the plant. I was overjoyed to see it—green, bulbous, sitting in the sun with staves upraised. It felt like an old friend welcoming me home from my blurry travels. I stood and looked at it for a moment as if to say "hello" and "thank you." Then I turned and strode confidently uphill in the direction of the lodge, turned left on the next street and proceeded forward. But there was no lodge in view.

What had I done wrong? I looked toward Teela as if she could tell me. I wished I had written my route down earlier, but even now that seemed a poor alternative. I retraced my steps back down to the original corner with the bank and the agave. Then Teela and I walked up farther to a second side street and turned left, walked down a long block, and there it was: the open gate, the wall, the glowing sun-baked building. I took Teela to relieve herself in a secluded spot near the car, then walked up the curving path to the front door. Feeling as if invisible trumpets were heralding my return, I stepped inside in time for breakfast.

I looked for Hannah to tell her I was back. A clerk at the desk said she was having her massage, so I entered the breakfast room and sat down at a side table. The morning sun filtered gently through a recessed window opposite me. I was eager to eat. I tied Teela to my chair so my hands would be free, then I stepped over to a table laid with breakfast foods, where I bent my head down to look closely at them. Gingerly, I picked up a couple of pastries and held them near my eyes and nose to determine what they were: was this a fruit-filled small pastry, a cinnamon-covered cookie, or a muffin? I tasted one blond pastry that turned out to be a piece of melon. I lowered my head down next to the two pots to find out which was the caffeinated coffee, which the decaf. As I poured my coffee, I put my finger in my cup to gauge when I had reached the top, but cautiously, trying not to get burned. I thought about how when Hannah is with me at buffet meals, I often ask her to tell me what the different foods are, but when alone, I explore in this close-up manner, much as I do when out on the street. I hoped Teela would not pull the chair she was tied to into the middle of the room while I took my time choosing my breakfast. Soon I brought my food back to the table and greeted Teela, who settled on the floor at my feet.

As I sat and ate, I looked out through the windows at the morning sun glowing on the patio outside. Then I stepped outdoors to see the sunlight more closely. It was a wonderful, soft, quiet yellow light. I stepped back in to get warm. Later, I told Hannah, "You have to go out on the patio right away to see the light." But

I think she just humored me by going out. I knew she really cared about the moon. She likes sunsets, while I like sunrises. With my eyesight fading, however, I was beginning to appreciate sunsets more. I wanted to become less afraid of impending darkness. At first when my eyesight began to fail, I would feel my day was over when darkness descended, that I might as well go to bed since I saw so little in the absence of bright light. But gradually, I had begun to continue my daily activities even when my surroundings grew dim—watering my plants in the yard in the darkness, knowing from memory where each one was. I began to feel more useful at night. Still the new light of day entranced me. It was my favorite time.

When Hannah returned to our room after her massage and soak, she looked glowing and satisfied. The woman who gave her the massage had once been legally blind, Hannah told me. She had recovered her eyesight, but during the time she was blind, she had learned to do many things by feel. When giving massages now, she did much of the work with her eyes closed, preferring it that way. She gave Hannah the name of a man in San Francisco who conducted workshops for people who could not see that encouraged a different kind of visualizing. That alternative felt familiar to me, and I was glad the masseuse had valued seeing through touch. For me, too, nonvisual techniques of touch and hearing often felt better and more pleasurable than relying on my eyesight.

Hannah soon checked us out of the lodge and I began carrying our bags down to the car. I felt as if a cycle had been completed, and it surprised me. The night before, which had been full of my worry and concern that I was in the wrong place, had turned into an adventure in hospitality and in making things work out despite my lack of sight. My morning walk, challenging as it was, had highlighted my abilities to find my way. It had given me a sense of triumph.

Down at the car, in what was left of the morning light, Hannah and I took pictures of each other by a wooden side gate in the earthen wall. We both looked happy.

We had lunch in the restaurant downtown where I had turned back earlier on my walk. Small children came over to look at Teela, who lay sprawled on the floor half under our table, but half out. Then we began our drive north. We were lucky, the clerk in the lodge had said this morning—the lake at Elephant Butte was low, so not many people were staying at the lodge. We were lucky in other ways, too, I thought. We were lucky that I was blind, for it brought Hannah and me together more, particularly when out in the world. It caused her to do all the driving when we traveled. At first, she had only done more of the driving; I still drove some, but after a point driving became too frightening for me. I now often chose to do what was safest. I was lucky that I realized I needed to work at seeing—both at having a positive perspective on my life and at deciphering what was in front of me. I had to be aware constantly of my surroundings and of how I moved within them, and I was always figuring things out, especially how to accomplish tasks in a new way. I was fortunate that I was traveling with a loving partner and with a guide dog on whom I was learning to rely. I had a moveable home. I was capable of appreciating things even if my sight was diminishing. I was not very good at counting streets. But perhaps that would change.

Chapter 6

Evening Lights

We drove north and the next night, Hannah had a treat in store for me. After dinner that evening, in the crisp cold of a black sky, we bundled into the car.

"Where would you like to go?" Hannah asked me.

I knew only that I wanted to see lights. For me, since the night is almost completely black, lights stand out in relief, glowing with a simple beauty, providing a view not complicated by subtle questions about what I see. Things are either light or dark, visible or not. Glowing shapes hang like artworks in the night sky. Especially in the desert at Christmastime, the bleakness, the cold, the expanses of black are suddenly decorated with streams of light—colored lights, white lights, perhaps luminarias. Hannah knew that on this night I wanted to drive around and see Christmas lights.

I looked now into the darkness of the parking lot surrounding me. Here and there ordinary lights glowed: taillights of cars, signs for gas stations and for restaurants, street lights. I could not see buildings in the dark unless they were lit, but I could see these lights, bright designs piercing the blackness of the night.

We drove across the highway and away from the restaurant where we'd had dinner—El Sombrero, identified by a hat with blue and red neon lights flashing—and headed toward the center of the town to which we had come specifically to see Christmas lights.

"Look over there," Hannah soon pointed in the darkness, "on your left. There are good lights there."

We were nearing the plaza in the old part of town. "What do you see?" I asked Hannah.

"Reindeer. A Christmas tree, a star, Santa."

I remembered that the year before, I had walked in this plaza quite close to the lights and seen the reindeer, the star, Santa, and a small crèche. I had been surrounded by white lights hanging above me outlining their shapes. But the lights tonight seemed not as bright as they had then, perhaps because they were too far away, or perhaps my eyesight was simply murkier.

"I want to see lights on houses," I told Hannah.

"I'm taking you there." She turned right. The night became darker. I looked into a great deal of blackness, interrupted by house lights shining through windows, the suggestion of Christmas trees inside. I saw shadows of low buildings spread along dark streets, a lone house surrounded by white lights, another with colored lights around a picture window framing a Christmas tree draped with blue lights.

Hannah turned left and went faster.

"Don't speed," I cautioned.

"I think I see lights down this block. I'm taking you to them." She slowed before a house completely outlined with white lights; it had lights on a fence in front and on bushes. There were lights on a home next door, but most of the houses in the area were dark.

Hannah turned back and headed out of the residential enclave toward more open space, then up a hill where suddenly there were bigger trees and larger homes. One house looked like several strung together, all portions of it outlined with white lights. A tree near the road was hung with lights. The wall had lights. Colored lights framed the front door. On the roof was a string of electric luminarias, glowing plastic versions of candlelit paper bags. I took out my binoculars to try to see them more closely.

"Good lights," I said to Hannah. "Find some more."

She turned, headed further into the wooded area and pulled into someone's driveway by accident; we were surrounded there by an electric glow—white lights from an overhanging car shelter and a tree nearby.

"More?" I asked, as Hannah drove further. "Look at that one," I exclaimed, seeing a house magically lit.

"It's the same house as we saw before," Hannah murmured. "This road is taking me in circles."

I smiled. I was pleased to be seeing all these lights, but there was something about being in a well-to-do area, something about the whiteness of the lights. I like colored lights best, the old fashioned kind, rarely seen anymore, the big bulbs that if one light goes out, it shorts the entire string. I especially like luminarias, not the plastic ones, but the paper bags with sand in the bottom anchoring a small white candle. Every time we drove around at night on this trip, I had hoped to see luminarias, but they were normally set out only on Christmas Eve. They needed tending. They were not like electric lights that you just turn on.

I was touched by Hannah's willingness to drive me around. Back at home, she had driven when I looked out the window at night to determine whether I could still see lights well enough to enjoy them, or whether my vision was now too dark. I wanted to know, would I be able to see lights when we visited the desert?

Hannah was driving us back now toward the plaza, a distant white glow; then she headed off in a new direction, spying something. Teela was quietly asleep on the backseat of the car, stirring occasionally when she heard my exclamations.

Here we were, I thought, as I jostled about, two women and a guide dog from California driving in circles in the cold of a winter's night, looking for Christmas lights so that one of us, the blind one, could be happy with her sight. But it was more than that. We were two Jewish women. Not only was I in a strange town, but a strange culture. Hannah was graciously driving us and, all the while, I was aware that she hated Christmas, or at least was made very uncomfortable by it.

Every year, as the holiday approaches and ads for it begin appearing on television, Hannah starts to become angry at the way Christmas invades and is so commercial and Christian. She wants to ignore it. She was raised as a Conservative Jew in a small town where her family's first question about a person was, "Is she Jewish?" and a distinction between "us" and "them" was vital. Christmas was for the goyim, for Christians, not for us. The idea was to keep it out of your house and your consciousness.

I was raised as a Reform Jew. I had learned that the pagans had defiled the temples of the Jews at this time of year. The Philistines had long ago overrun us. Chanukah was celebrated in defiance. This was a season to remember you were Jewish, not to run about seeing Christmas lights. There also was something, for me, about being born in the wake of the Nazis, something about my knowing that persecution should never be a surprise. To be Jewish was to tread lightly, look around always for the enemy, be concerned about your safety in non-Jewish lands. Yet for quite a few years now, I had been taking Hannah, in the wintertime, to a very Catholic part of the country where Christmas was very much in the air, and now, with my eyesight fading, I was taking her with an intense desire to see Christmas lights. Although I did not have Hannah's same resentment of Christmas, I had some similar feelings with which I tried to understand hers.

I grew up with neighborhood Catholic children who pointed their fingers and told me I killed Christ. At summer camp, when Protestant girls spoke disparagingly of Jews, I hid. My family was divided about Christmas. My father was an assimilationist Jew and thought it was an American holiday, to be celebrated "for the children," and that it represented world peace. My mother, who grew up Conservative Jewish like Hannah, was in tears each year when we celebrated Christmas as well as Chanukah. We would have presents on Christmas morning and then she would go into the kitchen and make latkes and cry. I always knew celebrating Christmas was not right for us. The words "Merry Christmas" never slipped easily from my lips. Chanukah never seemed a true substitute for the need to assert, "I don't. I can't. I'm different." As an adult, I have not celebrated Christmas, though I like the season, the festivities, the sweet cookies and cakes, the suggestion of home-like warmth. Nonetheless, each year I feel a tension as the date approaches, and on this drive, I felt it lurking in the background. I felt, at every turn, at each sighting of the wondrous lights, that Hannah was braving the Philistines in taking me around.

"The lights are pretty, don't you think?" I said, trying to be soothing.

"I'm glad you're happy, dear."

I am not sure if there is anything I do for Hannah that matches her willingness to drive me to see Christmas lights, anything for which I cross the same line, go against my deepest upbringing. As we drove, I was thinking about our pairing and about how much I enjoy the lights, despite feeling that I ought not. I don't put up Christmas lights myself, so I am beholden to others for their displays, and I feel as if I am partaking of other people's worlds. I am an outsider peering in through an invisible glass. It is similar to my experiences with my eyes: I walk around feeling I am in a strange land, more strange each day I set out. What will I see now? I wonder. Will it be the same as before? Better or worse? Will I enjoy what I see? What will they have set before me? It is new each time. I feel, too, that no one really knows what I see. I am from an unknown culture immersed in this familiar one, looking like I am simply taking my next step, lifting my fork to my mouth, saying hello; and, all the while, I am trying to figure out, "just what is this person's face, what is this breakfast food, this store, this object in front of me, and how do I get around it?" Because my disability is invisible, I have to assert repeatedly who I am, often in negative terms: "I'm blind. I don't see. I have a dog. I can't." And often I hide, as I did when a child. I do not want to call attention to myself and my difference.

I was thinking, too, as we drove through the night, that my

eyesight may be failing, but that does not mean Hannah should be doing all this extra for me.

She was driving us now toward very bright lights. The space ahead seemed to open out into broad flatlands where suddenly, there was a great glow. One house after another was lit, sending a diffuse whiteness up into the night sky. Hannah pointed. "You don't need to point," I told her. "I can see."

The sky seemed lit with thousands of lights, as if a truckload of them had been thrown down from above. But it was actually distinct sets of lights. First one house, then another, was outlined in white, and in color. The entire house before me was thus sharply outlined—the roof in white lights, the square chimney was edged in lights, the frame of a pointed mock-roof over the front door was lit. "What's that?" I asked Hannah, seeing a second small house. "It's the garage," she explained. "These people have lit up every-thing." I looked more closely, using my binoculars. Every bush in front of their house was lit. There were reindeer and trees and stars on the ground. Their cactus were lit, with lights hanging from their spikes. The agave out front had colored lights on its upraised swords. Each window of the house was framed with lights.

And this was not the only such ornately glowing home. The house next door was carefully draped—with colored lights along its roof, and around the garage and the windows, and on whatever odd plants were set out in front. The next house had blue lights; and across the street, the houses glowed. The display went on for several blocks on both sides of the street. One house had so many layers of lights it seemed to be in motion—white lights, and below them, colored lights flashing on and off, and on the roof and the front wall, close enough for me to see, were electric luminarias. I lifted my binoculars to my eyes. I put them away. I decided to pretend that the luminarias were real, that these electric plastic bags were brown paper and sand. My eyesight was so blurry that pretending was not hard. And I wanted to feel satisfied, to feel I'd seen what I wished.

"I saw them," I whispered to Hannah. "I saw the luminarias."

"I'll take you to see real ones next year," she promised.

We stopped the car and looked out, moved forward, stopped again. The houses looked splendid for as far as I could see. I could not see the shapes of the actual buildings unless I looked very hard beneath the bright outlines of their lights. "What do the houses look like that the lights are on?" I had asked Hannah at first.

"They're modest houses, tract homes. The bigger ones might be ranchstyle."

I was all the more moved that at night in the dark, the economics of the houses did not matter. The beauty was in the lights, in the eye of the beholder, in my eye, blinded to an advantage. Here, plastic could become real, modest homes rich with lights and with a willingness to put on a display for me—the blind visitor, the Jewish girl. The broad expanse of elaborate lights, of strings of glowing shapes and colors, decorations hanging in the night air, were so many and so generous that even Hannah finally murmured in agreement, "Yes, these are good lights."

I looked off into the distance ahead and remembered that a couple of years ago, we were driving in this area and I had seen a shooting star. It looked green as it whooshed through the black sky and was gone. Back then, I could still make out a falling star. Now this display, this airy carpet of lights would have to do.

Teela moved, waking from her sleep, and looked out the window. She got alert, licked her lips. She had seen a cat.

"Have you had enough?" Hannah asked me.

It was hard for me to believe it possible, but yes, I'd had enough. I felt I had seen enough lights for one night, perhaps for a long time to come. It was nice now to go back into the darkness, back to an uncertain future with regard to my sight. I had seen what I came for—the magical glow, the display, something I had not seen before, nor quite expected.

We drove now toward the highway, heading back to the small

town where we were staying. It was a town barely visible from the road—dark houses scattered on dark streets next to low-lying farmland near the river. I expected there would be lights on some of the homes as we drove past them. Hannah stopped in front of one. "Look," she said. "There are reindeer and farm animals in the front yard." But I could not see them. I saw only lights. The metal figures of the animals were just too dark. So I imagined them out there in the yard. Hannah drove past another home draped with white lights. These lights seemed not as bright as back in the town we had left. But they were soothing to me now, a denouement, a way of slowing down, of returning to the darkness. We pulled into the driveway of the house where we were to stay. A row of white lights hung from a low fence in front. The smell of a pine fire wafted from within, welcoming us. I felt that no one with normal sight could have enjoyed lights as much as I had that night, or could have appreciated, as much, the efforts of her guide. It was a long way, I felt, from the time of my morning walk in the sunlight the day before in Truth or Consequences. That bright morning, my vision had felt murkier than it did now when the darkness hid the degree to which I don't see. At night, the outer blackness hides my inner lack of sight. At night, I do not expect to see more than I can. I don't try as much to see. I relax more.

It was a long way from the glaring sunlight that bathed the road as we drove to Mexico, a long way from the Middle of No-where Bar and Cafe and my yearning for a spectacular sunset. I had been disappointed then, and now I was satisfied, and I was here with Hannah, and with Teela, carving out our own space—Jewish in a Catholic country, blind in a world of sight. It was a long way, I felt, from the restaurant across the border where the Christmas lights never came down, where that was the accustomed landscape, to here where the lights were new, set out only once a year—a challenge to my blindness, an antidote to my sadness.

This trip, it seemed to me, was scattered with many such lights in my darkness: when I first saw the mountain, Big Hatchet, and the desert basin around it that I did not expect to delight in; when I saw the glowing white plains that looked like snow by the road-side as we drove south; as I peered into the hazy light surround-ing the blurry town of Hachita. There was the cactus garden glis-tening in the late afternoon sun, and the artichoke-shaped agave that sat beside the bank in Truth or Consequences resplendent in the morning light, helping me find my way. Each of these visions was a light in my darkness, something special, something there for me. As was Hannah, always ahead of me or beside me. I saw her enveloped in a yellow-white glow leading me back carefully along the cracked streets of the town in Mexico, watching out for my safety. And Teela, golden, but beyond golden, soft, helping me not to fall or feel too alone.

The iridescent green hot tub in the Sierra Springs Lodge, the warm water speckled with the candlelight, that was certainly a light in my darkness. As was the hospitality of the staff, of those strangers who, like the woman in the trading post who ran home to bring me back her puppy, each reached out to me. Every time a person offered to help me because of my lack of sight, whether I had accepted the help or not, it had felt like a light to me—an acknowledgment of my presence, my reality, my blindness. So often people say nothing, not wanting to offend. And then I feel more strange, more outside, an invisible woman on the other side of a murky glass. The naming, the acknowledging, the offers all help.

Because so much is uncertain or invisible in my own field of vision, each time I finally figured out what things were as we traveled, the objects seemed to glow as with an inner light. When I looked for the gas station with both a tire gauge and air and found humor, when I finally identified the breakfast food on my plate, when Hannah told me the color of the water glass by the pool, when I recognized that we were in a disabled room—each of these moments glowed as if lit with an inner light—the light of discovery, of an unexpected find, of wresting something from the darkness. Where a moment ago, an object had been missing and a source of frustration for me, now it was found. I suddenly saw it, and I felt happy. These are everyday occurrences, these shining moments of recognition, and I did not have them as much before beginning to lose my sight. Perhaps such moments are reserved for the blind.

I was traveling now with Hannah in the winter desert and just being together was a great light in my darkness.

For me, there are many kinds of light, and I need to remember and value each one, all the more so as I become surrounded by increased darkness. The Christmas lights piercing the night sky reminded me of all the other lights. They reminded me that no matter what my initial sense of disappointment or loss, my experiences could be converted into highpoints, brightness, and unexpected satisfaction. I hope forever to keep an image of the night Hannah, Teela, and I drove around chasing Christmas lights, Hannah speeding off in search of a distant glow; me straining to see, yet delighting in my sight.

PART 3: SIGHTED AND BLIND

Chapter 7

Navigating Duality

I am blind and I am sighted. I am often not sure of what I see. Do I see what is there? The images look so small. People on the street at any distance seem tiny to me, with thin legs that disappear in the shimmering sun. Often the people themselves disappear if they are not in my direct line of sight. Cars on the street also look tiny, like toy cars in the distance. Up close, however, they appear so large that I must take them in piece by piece: a part of a fender, the blue oval emblem that says "Ford." Though I can no longer read the brand names, I still play the game of guessing at the makes of the cars as Teela pulls me quickly past them.

Walking down the street with her, and everywhere I go, I feel self-conscious. People see me with a large dog and they notice me. Sometimes they think I am blind and being guided by Teela. Other times they think I am sighted and training her for someone else who is blind. The uncertainty of how I am perceived makes me anxious. I must emotionally navigate my identity at the same time as I physically navigate my route.

The contradictions abound for me. For instance, I do not see well, yet I keep trying to; I look around intently with my eyes. My vision is impaired, yet I enjoy my sight. When I step outside with Teela and I am wearing my dark glasses, I am overjoyed by the images that come in through the tinted lenses by bright contrast—

a white edge of a house, a light tree trunk reflecting the sunlight, a set of large bright letters against the dark background of a store awning. Although the letters look bent and broken to me, and as if they are underwater, glowing with a phosphorescent shine, to me they are beautiful, magical. I stare at these letters and I think, "I can see." It takes many internal steps, much going over in my mind, to remind myself that I take such joy in seeing the letters precisely because I can't see, or can't see well. Objects that have some clarity come through the hazy confusion in front of my eyes and make me happy.

As I walk farther down the street, I pause to stare at a stop sign ahead. The letters on the sign's red background waver and disappear, then come into focus; I study them with my right eye, then my left, testing my vision, as I often do—trying to determine the exact state of my sight. Which eye is better now? Which sees with more of an edge? Has my vision changed since I last looked at this sign? I continue walking past pieces of sharpness, sections of buildings and streets. I know what I am looking at generally, but if I did not, it would seem a jumble.

Traveling in my familiar neighborhood in San Francisco, much like my more distant travels, is like being in a movie that I perceive in separate frames that do not flow smoothly into one another. In this choppy movie, I focus on what lies straight ahead, trying to make it out. A small figure down the street may be a child or a dog. I tilt my head, using the different parts of my eyesight in an attempt to bring the figure into focus, though it will only become clear closer up. Teela, stopping, points her nose toward a square object farther away. Odd-looking at a distance, it turns out to be a wheelchair that someone has left on the sidewalk. I stand beside it and examine the arm rests and wheels, taking them in one section at a time, much as I do when using a magnifier. Maybe I'll remember what a wheelchair looks like from a distance when I next see one. I pass the child and I wonder why I thought it was a dog. Why am I always seeing dogs? Perhaps because I overlay new objects with memories of familiar ones, making assumptions until I find out what is really there.

As I walk, deciphering the world—guessing at and identifying the different pieces of it—I am constantly thinking about what I see, and by this I mean not only what an object is, but what it means to see it. Does seeing a child the way I do, or seeing a person's thin shimmering legs in the distance, mean I am sighted? Does it mean I am blind? What does what I see say about who I am? Questions about my identity always lurk for me behind the more practical questions about what lies before me.

I see better now than I did a year and a half ago when the cataracts on my eyes had become extremely dark. Now that the cataracts have been removed, my surroundings are often so bright that I have to wear dark glasses when outside, where I used to rely on the darkness within my eyes shielding me from glare and the pain of too much light. Because I see better now, I often forget that I don't see. I stand in a supermarket and look up at the big letters on signs high in the air above the aisles, marveling that I see them, and then I turn and bump into a person at my side, invisible to me because she is lost in a blind spot in my peripheral vision. A few days ago, I was in front of my house playing Frisbee with Teela. I threw her floppy cloth disc up the sidewalk for her to retrieve and it hit a woman walking toward me, whom I did not see coming for she, too, was lost in a blind spot. More startled than she was, I apologized, and I vowed internally to be more careful in the future—a vow I often take when there is a mishap. I will cross a street, not see a car coming toward me, feel lucky it stops, then vow to be more careful—to listen as well as look in all directions next time. I'll walk into a tree branch overhanging the sidewalk and vow to remember where it is for the future. Or I will trip on a crack, then promise myself to remember it. I show Teela the broken piece of sidewalk so she will stop and alert me next time, but I also need to map the crack's location in my mind.

As Teela guides me along sidewalks, she halts at the curbs.

They look brighter to me now than they used to, but I still cannot make out the depth of a curb or the edges of steps. On some days, Teela and I climb a steep flight of stairs on a hillside behind my house. Coming down the stairs, even with her guiding me, I wobble, feeling uncertain of my balance because I can't see the edges of the steps. I fear I'll tumble down them. I have read that blind people do better navigating stairs entirely by feel; it's sight combined with blindness that makes the stairs confusing. But unfortunately, I am still holding onto my old habits of sight. It's easy to feel that my vision is reassuring, that my sight is a good guide, even when it is not.

I know I am not a good judge of distances and speed. When I sit in the car beside Hannah while she is driving, the forward movement of our car often frightens me. Other cars passing us on the highway from the sides seem to come out of nowhere. I cringe and pull back, suddenly seeing them. Will I be hit? I am always expecting an accident, and not only when in the car, but in all of my movements—especially in the intimate surroundings of our home. In our kitchen, for instance, I am very careful with knives and scissors. As I stand at a counter cutting a slice of bread, I must watch out not only for my fingers, but also for one of our cats, Shadow, who likes to leap from counter to counter. I fear she will fly through the air and land on the knife and I won't see her coming. I have already had a few close calls with her. Thus I put knives away quickly and always hold them point down. I sometimes tell Hannah to do the same, forgetting that she can see the cat.

Hannah and I have worked out several maneuvers for when we are both moving about in our kitchen—to compensate for my lack of sight, and so that I will not bump into her. "I'm coming behind you," she will say to me, "I'm on your right. I am going toward the cabinet."

I will often say the same to her when I move, because I am not sure she will be aware that I don't see her. I will be moving in a way that does not take into account that she is there, and I may move too quickly. What if she moves at the same time? I know I need to move slowly, but I don't always remember to do so. I keep attempting my old habits of speed as if quickness is a sign of ableness, when now just the opposite is so for me.

"Cat on your right," Hannah will call out to me while we are making dinner, thinking I don't see the cat sneaking up. "She's on the counter about to take your food."

But then sometimes I will see the cat. "I see her," I'll tell Hannah.

"I don't always know what you see," she says, feeling confused and a bit hurt by my rejection of her help. She's confused and hurt, as I so often am, because my sight comes and goes.

In our house, I often trip over one of the dogs or one of our three cats. I confuse the pets, too, because sometimes I see them and sometimes I don't. And always I think that I *should* see them. I should remember to watch out, to think about where they are, to step carefully. In addition to Teela, we have a small black poodle, Esperanza, and our cat Shadow is gray. Both pets are harder for me to see than Teela, with her light golden fur. Our two other cats are easier for me to notice because they have white feet and white bellies. Still I wonder, why can't I see them all, even the dark ones? Why can't I remember where they are likely to be and step around them, "seeing" with my nonvisual awareness, my sense of their habits, as blind people learn to do?

Clearly, whether I am at home or out, I am preoccupied by my sight. Do I see? Don't I see? Will I be safe as I move? Will others be safe around me? Is my vision better now than it was before? Or worse? Will it change again? I somehow believe that I am what I see, and that my value is determined by my sight. I worry that I will have less worth if I see better, and also if I see worse. Why these worries? Why must I so often remind myself that I don't see?

I am back in the supermarket, where I walk over to an aisle and stand for a long time staring at the shelves, searching for colors and shapes that are familiar. Taking out my pocket magnifier, I lean in close to one shelf to check a price, which I can't quite make out; there's not enough light for using my magnifier. I pick up a jar of salsa and hold it close to my right eye, looking through the small round plastic lens at the ingredients, trying to catch the light and to angle the lens carefully with the curve of the jar so the letters don't become distorted. It's a lot of work for a small item, yet this process has become natural to me.

Still, I feel self-conscious—for spending so much time and for taking up so much space in the aisle as Teela lies beside me on the floor and I try to figure out what I want to buy. Standing with jar in hand, I feel I should not be here deciphering this label, or trying to. A blind woman should have someone with her, or ask for a store clerk's help. But I have taken myself here. I am using my sight. I feel caught in the world of the sighted acting like I'm blind. And I wonder, am I acting? Am I sighted, or blind? How can I be both? The answer may be clear to others, but it's rarely clear to me. In part, this is because of the overwhelming power of my sight and the complex hiddenness of what I don't see. I find it hard to explain to others what it is like for me, and hard to see it myself. I find it hard to believe that I am blind when the standard for making that statement is so often assumed to be black and white: a person is blind or not, sees or does not, fits completely in one category or the other. Yet I see and do not see; it's very individual: I feel that no one else sees quite what I do, or misses out on exactly what I am blind to. My loss of sight has given me a new appreciation for the saying that we each see differently; it has given me a sense of the profound isolation involved in individual perception.

Although I often don't see, or I see something that quickly disappears or is distorted, I still think I should be able to do things as I did them before when fully sighted. I should be able to walk without a dog or a cane, drive a car, read without magnifiers, manage the light and somehow discern objects better. "Don't give up," I tell myself. "Don't ask someone else, don't act blind." At the same time, I know I try, in many ways, to act blind. I walk down the hallway in my house at night without turning on the lights, and instead touch the walls in the dark and feel for the openness of doorways. I step carefully through our unlighted living room, similarly feeling my way, touching the edges of tables, chairs, and lampshades. Reaching the front window, I draw the drapes against a world I can't see. In the morning, in the kitchen, I reach into a darkened cabinet, searching for a jar by feel. I often find something in this cabinet, or in Hannah's closet, that she won't be able to find by sight.

When returning from an afternoon out walking with Teela, I usually enter our house through the basement, but I don't flip on the light switch. Instead, I put my hand in front of me to feel for obstacles, and I walk slowly. As I feel my way, I tell myself I am preparing for the future when I lose more sight, and for places where there are no lights, or where the darkness is unfamiliar. I tell myself I am developing skills and good habits that will serve me later when I will need them.

Harder for me to comprehend is that I am navigating in tactile ways for the present—because my surroundings are often dim to me, and because I feel an increase in confidence when I find my way by feel rather than by my limited sight or by straining to see. When I stop relying on my vision, I feel relief. I feel prepared and capable as I walk through my dark basement or hallway without bumping into things and I fear reverting back to my older, more helpless habits, my sighted ways.

I often concentrate so determinedly on finding my way as a blind person that I become lost in the moment. I stand at the front door to the basement and take out my keys, feeling for their edges to know which to use, then I put my finger on the door lock to find the keyhole—focusing on my touch, a substitute for what once was my sight. Inside, passing the light switch, I concentrate on remembering where the garbage cans stand and where the edge of the rug begins. I touch the dryer as I pass it, feeling the coolness of the metal, pleased to have gotten this far without veering off course; then I climb the back stairs blindly to the kitchen, where I greet my small dog by bending to touch her before I see her. Entering the dining room, I touch a light bulb to see if the table lamp has been left on. It is daylight and I would have to strain to see the difference between the bulb's glow and the natural light. I don't want to try to see; I just touch.

I have discovered that I like to touch the textures of my surroundings. In my yard, I touch the leaves of the plants; I especially like the shiny feel of new growth. I don't like to wear garden gloves anymore, but to feel the graininess of the earth. I finger the petals of the flowers in my garden even as I wonder, am I touching them because I need to, since my sight is poor, or simply because it is joyful for me? I know I can look at a fuchsia blossom up close and see something, but the flower seems not to mean as much, and to be less fully there, if I don't touch it. The fuchsia has a rubbery outer shell and a crinkly, delicate inner skirt. My pleasure in feeling its texture adds a new dimension to my life. The flower feels more alive to me than its faded color suggests.

Still I wonder, why am I touching this flower? What am I doing for now, what is for the future? Far too often, I fear that I am an imposter, a woman with good sight wandering the streets with a guide dog, touching her hallway walls and her plants, groping the bathroom floor for a pill I have dropped and can't see; I am panicked lest my cats ingest it. My fears, are they from yesterday, when I saw less; from today, a brighter day; for tomorrow, dim again? Or from a long ago time when as a girl growing up, I learned to pretend to the world that I could manage and not be weak, or helpless, or who I was? I think I learned so deeply, when young, that what is natural to me should be masked that in the present I deny my lack of eyesight and my vulnerability. I question my legitimacy. I tell myself that I am not compromised in any important way, and I imagine I can see.

Simultaneously, I take steps to adapt to my blindness. I learn new skills for navigating and for appreciating my surroundings. I also concentrate on combating within myself the assumption that my vision is adequate, for acknowledging the reality is necessary for my safety and my self-concept. And often just when I get to the point of recognizing my blindness and feeling comfort with it, I step outside, where I must confront the challenging assumptions of others, who are less familiar with the ambiguities that I have come to know as I navigate an uncertain landscape where blindness blends with sight.

Chapter 8

Are You Training that Dog?

In the supermarket, I am carrying a basket with my jar and a few other items up to the checkout counter. I'm remembering the time I bought sauerkraut thinking it was applesauce. I am more careful to study labels now. I put my groceries on the moving rubber counter, holding Teela close at my side. As the clerk begins to ring me up, I hear a woman behind me in line speaking to my back. "Are you training that dog?" she asks. I flinch, feeling frozen to the spot. How do I answer her? Why does she assume from my back that I can see? Why is she talking to my back? I wonder. I am suddenly angry. I let a silence hang in the air, hoping the woman will come to her senses. Then I turn around. "I'm blind," I say. "She's guiding me."

"Oh how nice for you, dear," the woman says. "It must be a real help to have her."

"Yes it is," I answer, smiling, and turn to face the clerk.

"What's my total?" I ask him, since I can't read the amount on the electronic screen. In answer, he points to the screen.

"I can't see it," I elaborate.

He shakes his head, as if I should be making more of an effort. I can see his gestures because he is close to me and large, while the small, fine lines on the screen blur away.

"Can you please read the amount to me?" I finally ask him.

He takes a breath, expels some air in a gesture of exasperation, and reads me my total. As I begin to sign my name on the credit card receipt, he moves my hand up higher on the paper. I am convinced I can sign anywhere, that the exact spot does not matter, but I don't say anything. I move the pen to where he points on the scrap of paper and sign. I am thinking now about how accustomed I have become to using my credit card even for small amounts, because it is awkward for me to make change. It takes me longer than others to identify my bills and coins, and to manage Teela with my other hand, and I don't want to hold up the line. The incident with the clerk takes my mind off the "training that dog" question, though the woman who asked is still behind me.

On another day, I am walking past some stores. A man comes toward me and stops me. "Are you training that dog?" he asks. He seems concerned. Still, I feel he is prying, looking into my eyes. "No, she's already trained, she's guiding me," I say, walking on.

I go home and look at myself in the bathroom mirror, staring at my eyes, trying to see what others see. Outside, I put on my dark glasses, thinking they will protect me from people seeing my eyes, noticing that they move and seem to focus, and then asking me, "Are you training that dog?"

Later, I am standing in a drugstore at a counter when a man walks up and stands beside me. "Are you training that dog?" he asks. "She's working," I tell him. He walks away from me toward a display rack, then calls back and asks again, "Are you training that dog?"

"She's working," I call back.

"You didn't answer my question," he pursues it. "But are you training her?"

I don't quite believe what I am hearing. I am aware that I don't want to say to him directly that I am blind, so I speak of the dog and say, "She's working." I leave without answering his question to his satisfaction.

Ten minutes later and farther down the street, Teela and I

approach a bench in front of a bagel store where a young woman is sitting holding the leash of a puppy. Teela wants to nose forward and play with the puppy, but I won't let her. "Are you training that dog?" the woman asks. I am startled because I am now wearing my dark glasses to mask my eyes. "She's working," I say of Teela. The woman gathers up her puppy and pauses. "But are you training her for a blind person?" she asks.

It's the start of another day. I am walking down a residential street near my home, following Teela briskly along the sidewalk, trying to keep up with her fast pace. I begin to pass two men sitting on the top stairs of a house. One mumbles something in my direction. I can almost feel it coming. "Are you training that dog?" he calls out to me.

"What do you see?" I call back at him.

"I can see. I know what you're doing," he yells out. "You're training that dog!" His words follow me as I walk on not breaking stride, feeling proud of myself for talking back to him, and struck by the point that he does not see.

Returning from an errand on another afternoon, I am walking along a quiet sidewalk. A woman coming toward me begins to cross the street in front of me. She seems to have two small dogs on leashes running around near her ankles. I begin to think about how I will keep Teela close to me when I pass her. The woman starts to cross the street, and from the middle of it calls out to me, "Are you t–"

I sense the words about to come. So I look straight ahead and focus my gaze in a fixed stare so that my eyes won't move. I am determined to "act blind," to seem unresponsive to her presence, as if I don't know she is there, which I hope will make her think I don't see her. I put my foot out and feel for the curb in front of me, exaggerating the motion, almost taking a misstep.

"Oh," the woman says as she nears me, pulling her dogs over to the side to let me pass. I feel not entirely comfortable with my charade, but I am relieved not to have the training question completed.

I am standing at an intersection about to cross a busy street. A man walks up to me from behind and begins to talk to me. I step off the curb; he steps off with me, continuing to talk. "Is that a guide dog?" he asks. "Are you training that dog? I had a cousin who trained one of those dogs." As I hear him, I try to listen behind his words for the oncoming traffic. I need to pay attention to Teela. I don't want her to walk me into anyone while crossing the street. I have to give her clear signals with my hands and feet concerning our direction and when to step up and down on the curbs. If I talk to the man at the same time as crossing, I will distract Teela, who may mistake my conversation for a command. "She's a guide dog," I call back to him as I walk on.

I am out walking with Hannah in a different part of town. Teela is guiding me, so I am slightly ahead, with Hannah a few steps behind my right shoulder, enabling Teela to see to both sides. A man comes up quickly from behind us and cuts between Hannah and me. He begins keeping pace with me. "Are you training that dog?" he asks. "She's working," I say, trying to ignore him. But he tags along with me as if glued, leaving Hannah pushed aside. "I see them downtown," he continues. "Do you train her downtown? I know a lot about them, I saw it on TV." I walk faster now, trying to outpace him, unsure which is the greater indignity—his cutting in between Hannah and me or his relentless questioning.

I am a block away from my home. A man, who seems to live in the area, approaches me. "Do you train dogs?" he asks. "No," I say. "I see you around here with different dogs," he goes on. "Only two," I answer. "I have a small black poodle. I walk her using my cane. This one's my guide dog."

"What a beautiful dog," he looks down at Teela and smiles. "But I've seen you with lots of dogs. Are you sure it's only two?" At this point, I am wondering if perhaps I have been walking more dogs than I know.

I am crossing a supermarket parking lot with Teela and a friend. A man comes up to me, "Are you training that dog?" he asks, alcohol on his breath.

I am striding along a neighborhood street. Up ahead, I see a figure that turns out to be a woman walking while holding the hand of a child. As Teela and I walk past her, I hear the woman say to the child, "That dog is in school. He's being taught so he can go help a blind person." I want to stop and tell the child that I am the blind person, but I keep going.

I am walking past several construction workers standing in the open doorway of a garage. One man turns to the other, "That's a blind dog," he says.

I step out the door of a chiropractic office, where I start to walk down a flight of outdoor stairs. A man coming up the stairs on my left begins to speak to me. I suddenly start to trip on the top step, not seeing it well. I grasp for the handrail, quickly switching Teela's leash to my righthand side, feeling I look awkward. "That's a good working dog," the man says, "she knows her job." I am aware that Teela has not helped me right then, but that I have displayed the awkwardness people expect of a blind woman. I feel good that I am recognized as blind, but afraid because I almost fell, and I'm aware that I would be the same person even if I did not trip.

I am approaching a bus stop with Teela. I say to her, "Halt." A young man sitting on a bench looks up at me. "Excuse me," he says, "do you mind if I ask, is that your dog?"

"Yes," I say. "It may not look like it, but I'm legally blind. She's working."

"I'm legally blind too," the man says, "but I'm allergic to dogs."

"You should get a cane," I think but do not say to him. He is wearing dark glasses, like me, but I had not initially given it much thought. We board the bus, and as we sit next to each other chatting, he tells me he has a friend who has a guide dog. One thing that bothers his friend is that people ask him, "Are you training that dog?" Hearing this, I am surprised and relieved. I had thought it was only me.

Hannah and I have two guests visiting, one of whom is blind.

She has come with her guide dog. We walk down the street to a restaurant, each of us following her dog. As we sit talking over dinner, she tells me that where she lives, people ask her, "Are you training that dog?" I am elated. This is her fourth dog. She is more blind than I am, but she looks young and athletic. She is a lesbian and seems alert and in control, not the stereotype of a blind woman.

I am standing in a butcher shop waiting for my turn when a woman walks over to me. "You're training," she comments, not quite as a question. "She's working," I say. "Can I pet her?" the woman asks, simultaneously reaching her hand forward and placing it on Teela's head. "Don't do that," I raise my hand to push hers away. The woman draws back, takes a few steps away from me, then she walks up again. "She looks sad," she says of Teela. "She's not sad," I mumble to myself, thinking that Teela looks sad to this woman only because she can't touch her. I sense some aggression in the woman's statement, as if she is punishing me for not letting her pet my dog.

A man comes toward me on the street. "Training?" he says with a big smile, or I think it is a big smile, it sounds that way. I feel he is being too friendly, almost intimate. I shy away from the intimacy and keep going.

When I used a cane, I would get some similar public responses. One day when I walked up to a garage sale table on a sidewalk, as I stood fingering a saucepan, my white cane leaning up against my left shoulder, a man called out to me from in the street, "You're not blind." Then he called again, "You're not blind," along with something else I could not make out. He sounded angry. I felt hurt and thought I had better not finger garage sale items anymore. From then on, I began to feel defensive in public, bracing myself for the next challenge about my sight.

Not long after that incident, I was passing a group of school children who were waiting at a bus stop. One of them, a girl, called out in my direction, "You can see," and like the man, she repeated it. I kept walking. I hoped that I hadn't heard her correctly, but I had. Soon I began to fear that I would be attacked while walking, that someone would come up and physically assault me for seeing.

Similarly, when people ask me, "Are you training that dog?" I feel attacked, pried into, challenged, as if I am being told, "You're not blind, so what are you doing with that dog?" The question implies that what I see is more important than what I do not see. The person asking, I suspect, is disappointed to find that I am not totally blind. If I were, they could have the experience of witnessing someone assumed to be truly different; they could marvel at how I got around despite my handicap. I don't like to disappoint. Perhaps people tend to see the ways others are like them, thus they don't see me as different; and the more physically capable I am, the more they don't recognize me as disabled or see the ways that I am blind.

I am walking one weekend morning with Teela when we come upon a car parked across a driveway. A man calls out, "There's a car there" and rushes forward toward me, lifting an arm as if to grab me and guide me around the car. "Thank you, I'll be fine," I say, nodding toward Teela, trying to indicate that I have a dog here whose purpose is to guide me.

Another day, a white truck is parked across a driveway. As I approach it, a workman calls out, "There's a truck there. I'll move it." "Thank you, no need to. I'll go around it," I say. At this point, I am beginning to feel bad for seeing the truck, as if I ought not. Yet a truck, especially a white one, is big, and when right in front of me, I do tend to see it. Furthermore, the way I have been taught to walk with Teela means that she takes me right up to the truck. Then she stops and shows it to me. I touch it. I tell her, "Teela, right." She then leads me along the side of the truck to the edge of the sidewalk, where she stops at the curb. I feel it with my foot. "Forward, left, left," I say, instructing her to guide me out into the street, around the end of the truck, and back to the curb on the other side, where she waits for me to feel the up-curb. Then I say, "Teela, forward." I step up over the curb and we continue in the direction of our original movement. This is a complex set of motions, not all of them evident to observers. There's no way, I'm thinking, that the workman with the truck can know what I am doing. Still, I wish he did know. When offered help like his around parked vehicles or when crossing streets, I feel patronized and treated as more incompetent than I am. But I also feel recognized as a blind woman and I feel cared for.

Sometimes when I walk down the street, people will call out simply, "What a beautiful dog." When they do, I assume they are recognizing me as blind. Maybe they are not, but because they are not saying "Are you training that dog," I jump to the conclusion. It is a compliment to hear them say that Teela is beautiful, and it makes me happy. Though I often wonder, "What about me? Aren't I beautiful too?" My point is that when I am out, people are always speaking to me. They talk about the dog, yet I experience it as about me.

I am standing at a curb. A woman catches up with me from behind. "I have a retired guide dog," she says. "That's nice," I say, "they are wonderful dogs." As she starts to talk to me about her dog, I get sad, thinking of Teela's eventual retirement.

Later I am walking uphill toward my home. A dark truck seems to have stopped in the middle of the street to my side. A man calls to me from the truck, but I am not sure what he's saying. It sounds like "Are you training that dog," but it could be "Nice dog." I don't know what to do or if he is even really talking to me. The truck edges forward. I finally stop walking. The man calls out, this time more clearly, to tell me that his brother has raised a guide dog or is thinking about it. "That's a beautiful dog," he says.

I am in a coastal town waiting for Hannah on a sidewalk outside a Mexican restaurant where she is ordering our takeout lunch. A man walks over to me. "Are you training that dog?" he asks. I explain that she is already trained. "I don't see very well,"

I say to the man, thinking to myself, why can't I simply say, "I'm blind?" I become determined not to look up at people on sidewalks in the future. Then maybe they won't feel they have eye contact with me and they won't talk to me. I often give eye contact without my knowing, since I will see the shape of a person's face, but because the features are blurred, I will not realize that I am staring into their eyes. Such contact invites response, even when I do not want it.

When I first got Teela and people began asking me, "Are you training that dog," I answered by saying, "No. She's already trained." More questions would follow: "What's her name? How long have you had her? How old is she? She looks like a nice dog. You're very lucky. How long was her training?" I would have to engage in a conversation to answer these questions. Some days I got asked if I was training Teela almost every time I went out. The "Are you training" inquiry soon began to anger me, which was my way of putting up an emotional armor in the face of what felt like assaultive words. To avoid being questioned, I began wearing my dark glasses even when I did not need them. I started to avoid looking directly at people, adopting a fixed gaze, or looking down at the ground, stumbling, or leaving a silence after the question, as if I had not heard it or did not think it was intended for me. I would look to the side of a person's face when we spoke, trying to appear more blind than I was. I tried wearing no glasses, distance glasses, wrap-around dark glasses. But people asked me anyway. Although my dark glasses looked opaque to me, I soon realized that people with normal sight probably saw my eyes through them, noted that my eyes moved, and then assumed that I, too, could see.

More than my physical acts, I considered the words of my answer to the questions. Initially, I had responded by saying of Teela, "No, she's already trained." But I never liked starting the conversation with "No." It seemed too negative for a social interaction. I also wanted to be more honest and direct in my answer. For I immediately heard, in the training question, a statement not about Teela, but about me, as if I was being asked, "Are you blind?" or, at least, "Why do you have this dog?" I wanted to respond to the undercurrents. So I decided I would bluntly tell the questioner, "I'm blind. She's my dog. She's guiding me." This answer was hard for me to say, but it felt good because I was speaking up for myself, rather than internalizing a judgment that felt untrue. But then I began getting the response, "Oh, I didn't know. Your eyes look healthy." Or, "It looks like you can see." The questioners were probably explaining themselves to me, but it felt like a challenge that required me to explain myself even further—to describe the exact details of my eye condition to clarify why it was not visible.

In time, I reverted back to speaking most often of the dog. It's awkward to speak of myself in answer to strangers on the street. My most common line has become, "She's working," and then I try to walk on.

At some point, I softened my self-identification by saying, "I'm legally blind" before saying, "She's my dog. She's guiding me." Or, I'd start out by saying, "You may not be able to tell by looking, but I don't see very well." That way, I could acknowledge the validity of the person's assumption that I could see. But when I answered in this less challenging way, I still heard the missing word in my mind, the more direct, "I'm blind. She's guiding me." And I wanted to say it again but feared I did not have the right.

So I began talking to myself as I walked along. "I am being guided by a dog," I would say in this inner conversation. "I am going to all this trouble with how I walk because I do not see, not because I do see. I am in the category of the blind; I'm on the other side of that line that distinguishes those who can take their vision for granted from those who can't. I was hit by a car I did not see coming. Think about all those times you almost fell," I tell myself, "think of all those close calls with cars;" and as I walked, I would see them again—the cars turning toward me, the accident when I was hit, my falling on the sidewalk, my glasses going flying, my missing curbs. I am saying that as I walk, I have learned to make myself materialize as a blind woman in order to counteract the aggressive public feedback I hear in the question, "Are you training that dog?" As I walk, I reinvent myself, reminding myself that I have to be careful and that I must engage in many additional maneuvers because of my blindness, including those of dealing with my inner emotions in response to public questioning.

Despite my efforts, however, the repeated external "you're not blind" has had the effect, like water on a stone over many years, of eroding my self-confidence. Because the questioning I receive can make me invisible to myself, my repeated attempts to assert my blindness are crucial for me, both my larger attempts like speaking to others, and the smaller, more invisible efforts that occur in my inner conversations.

I already know that I am sighted. That view has been ingrained in me since birth. My blindness is a new identity, quickly given, then almost taken away, invisible much of the time. Why do people assume sightedness when faced with a blind person? Why do I? I assume it because, like others, I have learned deeply that to be blind means not to see at all, to stumble, to fall, to need help, to suffer the handicap of lack of sight, that it means a condition that is both total and disabling. Sometimes I do stumble, sometimes I fall, sometimes I see, but at other times, I do not. When I think about why my blindness so often goes unnoticed, I consider, too, that the clues that point to it may be subtle—a difference in the harness that Teela wears that indicates she is a guide dog, a difference in how I act at curbs, a cautiousness, a hidden watchfulness, the suggestion of my terror on stairs.

There are many people like me—invisible people whom I pass on the streets—and I don't know they are blind unless they take out a pocket magnifier in a store, hold close the arm of a companion while crossing a street, ask a clerk to read their total at a checkout counter, carry a cane or follow a dog, stare for a long time at a grocery shelf, or wait for a traffic light to come around fully to their turn. And often, I will not see these other blind people, so focused am I on my own next step, my efforts to perceive the shapes and objects around me. I am limited by the constraints of my own vision. Yet I often walk quickly, following Teela, striding down sidewalks near my home, my head held high, appearing more confident than I am. People turn and ask, "Are you training that dog?"

Chapter 9

Airport Stories

I am at an airport on my first trip alone with Teela. Checking in at the United terminal in Los Angeles for a flight to San Francisco, I ask the clerk to confirm that I have the bulkhead seat I have re served to allow room for Teela to lie on the floor.

"I can't let you have that seat," the clerk says to me. "It's in our emergency exit row. Passengers sitting there have to be able to read and follow directions and help other passengers in an emergency."

"But I reserved it," I tell her.

"I am changing you to a different seat," she says.

Standing opposite her across the counter, I am thinking that I can follow directions, though I know I cannot read small print. Perhaps someone can read the print to me in advance. I know I can help other people.

"I reserved the bulkhead because I am traveling with a guide dog," I say to the clerk, pointing to Teela. "She needs room to lie down."

"We can't seat you in that row," the clerk says again and then begins to read to me from a formal statement about passengers in exit rows needing to have the ability to follow directions and assist others in the event of an unforeseen disembarkment.

I now begin to feel self-righteously angry. I am blind, not dumb. I don't want to be denied any of my rights. I don't want to be treated as less than I am. I hate that people are always thinking that blind people cannot do things. A cool-headed blind woman would be excellent at helping people out of the plane, I think, conjuring an image of a very capable blind woman opening the door and assisting others out, though I doubted that I would be that cool-headed in the circumstance. But Teela might be a help. I imagined her marching forward, leading people to safety from the downed plane.

"You can't deny me my seat," I say aloud to the clerk. "It's discriminatory."

She looks at me blankly, shakes her head, then begins typing on her computer keyboard, seeming flustered. I am surprised that I have used the word "discriminatory." It just tumbled forth, as if on its own. So I repeat it.

From the other side of the counter, the clerk finally hands me my boarding pass, assuring me she has changed it back to my original assigned seat in the bulkhead row. Her head was down and she was typing furiously as I walked away.

After passing through security, Teela led me toward the gate. When the plane was ready, she bounded down the ramp with me in tow. We stopped at the crack that separates the carpeted walkway from the entrance to the plane, where I always fear catching my feet; I took a big step. Inside, I asked where my seat was and went over to it. As I was about to sit down, a male flight attendant rushed over, reaching out a hand to stop me from sitting. "You can't sit there," he said.

"But it's my seat. I confirmed it at check-in. I need the space for the dog."

"This is the emergency exit row. You have to be able to open the door and help other passengers," he said.

"I can do that."

"I'll give you another seat with plenty of room for the dog."

My blood was beginning to boil. I was also beginning to think that I might not, in fact, be capable of helping other people off the plane. But I was going to insist. I looked toward the exit door. "I don't want another seat," I said to the attendant. "I can follow directions. I can help people just like anyone else can. It's discriminatory not to let me have this seat."

"Please," he said. "I can give you space for your dog. I assure you there will be plenty of room for your dog. You can have two seats, just farther back."

I looked behind me in the empty plane. It was a slow Saturday night. "This plane's going to be nearly empty," the flight attendant noted. "I'll give you a whole row to yourself if you want. You can pick your row."

I stood, not moving. He walked off to consult with someone or to call the front desk. Then he returned and stood beside me. "I can't let you have that seat," he said sternly. "We can't have wheelchairs in that row or anything that blocks the aisle. Your dog will block the aisle."

I gave up. I let him lead me back to another row, where he spread his hands and indicated I could pick my seat. As I sat down, I thought, with some relief, that at least now it was my dog who would block the aisle, rather than my stupidity.

Teela lay at my feet on the floor with plenty of space. The plane was so empty that if there was going to be a crash landing, there would not be many people to get off, and there was no one now sitting in the exit row to assist them. I began thinking about an imminent crash landing, and I could not help but think that perhaps I had forfeited my rights too soon, but at some point you just give up.

When I arrived back at my home airport, I waited at the gate for Hannah. She had promised to meet me there, since this was my first trip alone with Teela and I was worried that the airport corridors would be confusing. The airline had informed me that a disabled person or a child can be met at a gate if the person meeting them goes through security. However, there was no Hannah waiting for me. My cell phone soon rang. "They wouldn't let me meet you," Hannah said. "I'm waiting up in front. I'll watch for you at the elevator."

"Why wouldn't they let you come to the gate?" I asked her. "You're supposed to be able to."

"They said you gave up your rights to be a disabled person in Los Angeles. There was an argument with a clerk at the check-in counter and you gave up your disabled status. Since you're not disabled anymore, I can't meet you."

I flashed back to the clerk typing into her computer as I left. She must have been writing it all down for the record. Still, hadn't I retrieved my disabled status on board the plane when they changed my seat? It was hard to keep track of this elusive identity.

I smiled as I met Hannah outside the elevator. "Next time, I'll know," I said.

I have found airports to be less hostile than the experiences I face on the streets when people ask me, "Are you training that dog?" They are places primarily where I have to insist on my rights, even if I think I should, for the moment, suspend them. I'll wonder, why not let the airport staff change my seat or touch my dog? But some things seem too important to overlook—those having to do with my personal needs for dignity and space.

I was in the San Francisco airport standing in a security line on another of my early trips with Teela. When I got up to the table near the conveyor belt, I held Teela close to me, grasping her leash in one hand. With my other hand, I started taking off my backpack and my belt and emptying my pockets. Then I bent down to take off my boots, Teela's nose right down there with me. I put my boots into the bin on the table above me. When I had asked the security guard if I could go directly to the adjacent area where Teela and I would later be examined, he had said no, I should wait in the line first. Standing there now, I watched my belongings disappear out of sight on the conveyor belt, worried that I would never see them again, not seeing far enough ahead to keep track of them.

Someone ushered me toward the metal detector archway. I told Teela to go forward, remembering that, at guide dog school, they had told us not to let the security people separate us from our dogs. I should follow Teela through the archway first. The metal parts of her leather harness and her collar would set off the alarm. Then I should tell her to lie down on the other side of the metal detector, step back through it myself, and, while extending her leash full length, walk forward again through the archway, hoping not to set off the alarm this time. As instructed, I now left Teela on the other side of the scaffold, stepped back and went forward again, and when I walked through the detector the final time, the alarm remained silent.

Safely on the other side of the archway, I asked the security guard if he would like to inspect Teela's harness. I reached down and lifted it off her so he could check it for drugs, or knives, or any contraband I might have hidden in it, though I did not want to part with Teela's harness any more than I wanted to part with her. The guard took the harness and carried it toward the X-ray machine. "You can wand it," I offered.

And suddenly I recalled my very first airline trip to New Mexico with Teela and Hannah. On our return, in the Albuquerque airport, I had reached down too quickly and removed Teela's harness, unclicking it swiftly and expertly, proud of myself for knowing how to do it. Then I had felt a guard's hand reaching toward mine to grab my arm. "You shouldn't have done that," she said. "Now that you have, we're going to have to wand you." She took her phone out of the holster on her belt and called to someone.

Another guard then came over. "I'll have to feel around on the dog's body," he said, moving his fingers toward the soft fur of Teela's neck.

"Don't touch my dog," I almost barked. "You can wand her, but you can't touch her. That's why I gave you the harness. They didn't touch her in the airport on my way here. They got down on the ground and looked under her."

The guard then got down on his hands and knees and stared up at Teela's belly.

Teela stood patiently. She was ready to play, I felt, if someone started to touch her. If they handled her, it would distract her from her subsequent work of guiding me in the airport. She would think airports were places to go up to people and ask for petting.

I stood waiting. A managerial level security guard in a suit then came over. "Come with me," he said, motioning, and he spoke in a conciliatory manner. He led me to an area of seats and small tables. "Put your things there," he gestured. "I'll take those," he reached to lift off my backpack. Then he reached to take Teela's leash from me.

"You can't take the dog," I said.

"Okay," he stepped back. "But we'll need to examine you." He pointed toward the footprints on the floor.

"You have no right," I said. "I went through the security line. "I didn't set off the alarm. You are putting me through extra steps just because I have a guide dog."

"It's because you touched that–" he pointed to the harness. "You could have put something up your sleeve. I know you didn't. But we have to go through procedures."

He then motioned to a woman guard to join us. She asked me to spread my arms and legs, and then she wanded me. She touched the various areas where there might be a bulge, and where the metal rivets in my pants set off the beeper. I took my magnifier out of my pocket and handed it to her so she could wand it, even though it was totally plastic. I took off my boots again.

"The dog," the manager said.

"You can look under her, but you can't touch her," I said.

Only in retrospect do I realize that I have more stealthily guarded Teela's right not to be touched than I have my own.

When examined in the Albuquerque airport, I felt embarrassed about making such a fuss, but I still thought it wasn't right for them to put me through the extra scrutiny. I wasn't being treated like everyone else. Perhaps this particular airport was behind the times and they wouldn't always require a second exam. I heard one of the guards tell the manager as he walked me over that this was the first time they had encountered a guide dog, and they'd have to learn how to do it.

The odd thing is that since that first time when I was asked to spread my arms and legs, I have become used to the treatment. Now I ask to go over and sit on the side and wait for a security person to come and examine Teela, and not touch her, and then to examine me, allowing the touching.

When I tell people not to touch or pet Teela, I say it is because it will distract her from her work, which is true, but it's also because I feel it enables her to walk through the world safely, feeling it is hers, especially when she is on the other end of that leash attached to me. It must be a nice feeling, I think, probably because I myself walk around feeling quite unprotected—with my blindness, and having it signified so blatantly with Teela, and before her, with a white cane. People so often reach across into my space with their "Are you training that dog" question, and at airports, with the desire to examine me doubly—to make sure that I am not hiding something.

I have an image of myself walking with Teela down the many corridors we have, by now, traversed in airports. She guides me quickly, so we stride by the other passengers walking to their planes. As she leads me, I am always trying to keep my balance and not look foolish in the face of her exuberance, increased now with the excitement of the airport. I am watchful because it often is not clear to me whether Teela will bump me into other passengers as she weaves me through them. She is supposed to leave enough space for both of us to pass people, but sometimes she doesn't calculate for me on her right side. Then I'll bump into someone with my right shoulder. I keep trying to teach her not to bump me into people, but our working together is an imperfect art. She doesn't see people as unyielding obstacles.

In airports, too, I am especially aware that I have only one hand free when I am holding her harness, and it is not really free, for at any minute I might have to use it to take up the leash and give Teela guidance. I have to be very careful if I am carrying a cup of coffee or a sandwich so that I don't spill or drop it. I am constantly self-conscious about looking like I can't manage this process with style, about appearing discombobulated to people. This concern follows me as I follow Teela, as I try to move as if I know what I am doing, that I can navigate without tripping or spilling. At the same time, there is the signaling power of doing so—letting others know that I am blind.

People do not realize how much work goes into being attached to a guide dog. I try to make it look easy, and it's not that it is so hard, but it is time-consuming and attention-requiring. I am two people all the time. I can't forget Teela, except for sometimes when we are outdoors walking alone, without obstacles or impediments, and I am looking up into the sky at the big shapes of clouds, and taking in the fresh air. But inside places like airports, it is more like a hothouse. There are usually no other dogs, and people notice Teela, and they notice me, at least from the knees down. Fortunately, I can't see them looking at me most of the time. I can't see their eyes or expressions, and I am usually focused on my own navigation, so I am spared the specificity of being watched. But still I feel it.

Hannah tells me that when we travel together, she has noticed that people burst into smiles in the airport when Teela and I walk past them. They are happy to see a dog. That's been reassuring to me.

Once when Teela was leading me through a baggage claim area, she pulled me sideways and would not lead me to the door as I instructed. She was taking me to a small dog in a carrying case. Since then, I think she always looks for other dogs in baggage claim areas. I don't always have a bulkhead seat on the planes, but I try for one. Each time I fly, I find myself insisting that the security people not touch Teela. And each time, they want to. At one point, I decided to tell the security guards that she was a very nervous dog, so it would not be a good idea to touch her. "I don't think she'll bite," I said, seeking to imply the opposite.

"We understand," the guard drew her hands back.

I have also become used to the conversation that occurs in airports when I am sitting in the examining area with my shoes off, waiting for a security guard to come wand me. I will get the question, "Are you training that dog?" Once when I had just put on my shoes and was ready to be on my way, a woman security guard spoke up, "You must be training."

"I'm legally blind," I told her.

"You look like you can see fine," she said.

"It's not what it looks like from the outside," I tried to explain, pointing to my eyes. "It's how it looks from the inside." But I don't always have that much presence of mind.

Not long ago, when Hannah, Teela, and I were traveling cross-country to visit Hannah's family in Pennsylvania, we had to change planes in Atlanta. Before boarding the connecting flight, I needed to find a place for Teela to relieve herself. At the gate, I spoke to an attendant, "Can you call someone to take me to an outdoor area where my dog can relieve?" I asked.

"They won't come," he said. "We're understaffed. But I can call a wheelchair for you."

"I don't need a wheelchair. I requested a person when I checked in."

He thought a moment. "I'd let you out right here," he offered, motioning to the ramp behind him. "But the last one we let out ran away. We can't do that anymore."

I had images of Teela bounding off across the tarmac. "Can you call customer service for me?" I asked.

"They won't come here. But you can go there yourself. Or

you can just take her out the front door of the airport yourself." He pointed in the direction of a walkway.

"Exactly where is customer service?" I asked. "I can't see where you're pointing to."

"Back there, after the overpass."

"Exactly where after the overpass? Is it on the left or the right? Can you give me more specific directions?"

"On the left. After you pass the escalator, turn left to the overpass and it will be on your left."

Hannah, Teela, and I set off. At customer service, we found a long line of people waiting. I wanted to go right up to the desk and tell them that my dog had to pee, but I waited. A roaming customer service representative walked down the line asking what people needed. "I need someone to take me to an outside area where my dog can relieve herself. Then I need help back so I can have priority through security." The representative went on to the next person.

Hannah nudged me soon after that. "They want you up in front," she said. "They were waving to you, but you didn't see them. Go straight ahead to the desk."

At that moment, I was more surprised by the fact that I had not seen the airport attendants waving to me than by the fact that they were waving to a blind person with a guide dog. And I thought I should have seen them. I tend to forget that I see mostly what is straight ahead, not objects on the peripheries of my vision or in my blind spots. In airports, too, I feel surrounded by increased darkness. At the same time, the glare from the lights and the indistinct activity of people moving around confuses me. I am more nearsighted than usual because I don't wear my glasses, since they correct only to a limited degree and I don't want people to think I see more than I do. I am very aware of my visual impairments. Still, I am often surprised by my lack of sight, and I feel responsible for it, as if I should have seen those people gesturing to me.

I walked up to the desk and explained my situation.

"No one's free to go with you right now," the customer service attendant said. "You can take your dog out the front door yourself."

I began stuttering. It was a big airport. I would have to get on and off a train. "She really needs to pee," I said, pointing to Teela and conveying an anxiousness. "I would hate to get on the plane without taking her out—" I looked at the ground and stood very still.

In the back of my mind, I knew that Hannah had offered to guide me and Teela to the airport's front door, but I had declined. I needed to know I could do this myself: that I could ask for help in an airport and be given it. For the next time, I might be traveling alone.

Finally, a customer representative appeared. A large man in a uniform, he walked up and offered me his arm. I told him to go ahead, my dog would follow him. So Teela followed the man, I followed her, and Hannah followed me, all of us walking briskly single-file through the airport. The representative led us down corridors, through a back door, onto a service elevator, and into the basement, then onto a train for several stops, and off, and out into a lobby and to a side door. There, Teela and I stepped out into the warmth of the sunlight. The attendant pointed to a grassy area in a corner. Teela led me over to it, sniffed the grass and the scent of many before her, and peed. I marveled that I was ever expected to get here by myself.

The uniformed man led us back inside. He stepped to the front of the security line and spoke to the guards while I stood waiting next to a table. Hannah was somewhere out of my sight. A bin was handed to me. I took off my backpack, my belt, and took out my computer and placed these items in the bin; then I bent down to start untying my shoes. Suddenly, I heard "Over here" being called out in my direction by several voices. I looked up and saw blurry motions of white-shirted arms waving to me in the distance. They were on the other side of the metal detector, motioning me over. Teela guided me toward them. Then she stood while the guards gave her a cursory once over and under look. The guards told me to walk back and then come forward again through the metal detector, and I was processed through, mercifully quickly. Hannah stood on the other side of the archway, her eye on my belongings.

I got Teela ready and we were off again, following the representative, then on our own, back down the walkway, on and off the train, onto an elevator, up out of the basement, through corridors, and to the gate.

At the gate, I finally caught my breath. Teela had peed and we were all now safely back in time for our connecting flight. But it hadn't been pleasant—neither the rushing through the airport, through surroundings I couldn't see, nor my sense that I could not find my way alone, nor my need to insist, over and over again, that I should have assistance.

Airports—they are so very public and I am so very private, and so obvious with Teela. I feel odd being guided by a dog, trying to do it in good form yet looking like I'm blind. I am unsure of what others see, unsure of what I see myself, doubtful inside of who I am, and of what I should be doing all the while as I am doing it, as Teela pulls me forward and I follow her.

She weaves me through the other passengers, the world whizzes by me out of focus and I wonder, am I doing it right, am I blind enough? Do I need this dog? But if I let go of Teela's harness for even a moment, if I lose her, she then turns back and looks strangely at me, as if to say, "Where are you? You're supposed to be on the other end of this." I pick up the harness handle and start again the rolling walk we share, feeling it is worth it. If not for Teela, I would need a cane. People have to know I won't see them. Or they will think I am rude when I bump into them or don't give them the right of way. I don't want to be hit by something I do not see coming, or trip and fall, or collide with a person or object not in my direct line of sight. I now feel unsafe without a probe or guide in front of me, Teela far preferable to a cane.

On our return trip through the Atlanta airport, we had less time than on the outbound flight. I wanted to avoid rushing through the airport to get Teela to a spot where she could relieve herself. We were arriving on a small plane and I remembered that on our outbound trip, a similar plane had deposited us on the airport tarmac. It was night and dark then and I had not expected a set of rickety outdoor stairs would be rolled up to the plane. As I stepped down them, I was afraid for my footing. The engine noise outside was loud and I was worried about Teela's sensitive ears. At the foot of the staircase, I asked the attendant where to go. He raised his left arm and gestured. "Over there," he said. "Do you need me to take you?"

"No," I had answered instinctively. I did not want to take him away from his position at the foot of the staircase helping other passengers. "Just give me directions," I said.

"You go over to that building," he gestured again. "You sure you don't want me to take you? There are inside stairs."

"No," I said. Then I headed off into the dark by myself, the first person off the plane, terrified by the noise overhead, blinded by the brightness of the lights as well as by the darkness, and worried about Teela's ears. Would she be scared? Would she know where to go? We walked forward. I ducked under a parked plane. Where was the building I had so proudly announced I could find? Finally I saw an opening to my left. We hurried over. Inside, the staircase leading up looked black. I was convinced I could not climb it, and that I shouldn't ever do this again—say no to an offer of assistance at night outdoors in an airport.

From that experience, however, I now remembered that when we disembarked in Atlanta, I would exit onto the tarmac. I also remembered that when we arrived before, the gate attendant had suggested that other dogs had peed there. As soon as we landed this time, I climbed down from the plane and asked the attendant standing at the foot of the staircase, "Can you take me to a spot near here where my dog can pee?"

"Certainly," he reached and took hold of my arm. I shook free of him. "I'll follow you," I said, touching his arm gently instead, and walking beside him, heeling Teela at my left. He led us away from the plane for a distance, then stopped, gesturing that I could find a spot. I was on my own from here.

The airport tarmac was noisy, though this time it was daylight. I took a few steps forward, ducked under a plane, and followed Teela. Beneath the plane, a pile of leaves and papers blew in the wind. Teela headed for the pile, distracted by it. I worried about the engine noise around us and the fact that she had never peed under a plane before. She sniffed the pile of scraps. I bent down and unhooked her harness and extended her leash to full length so she could circle around me, in the routine way that signals that this is the time and place to "do her business." The movement stimulates her system. She circled, stopped, sniffed the leaves, circled again, then dutifully squatted and peed. Though that was all, it was the important elimination that I had worried about for the long plane ride home. I brought her back close to me by shortening her leash, slipped her harness over her head and her back and hooked it up under her chest. Then I almost had to drag her away from the interesting pile of dirt.

As we stepped out from under the plane, I squinted into the sunlight, looking for the attendant. Suddenly, he was in front of me with several people from the plane standing behind him.

"We were rooting for her," he said. "What kind of dog is that?"

I had forgotten about my privacy—that I probably didn't have any. Though I had not really forgotten. While under the plane, I kept worrying that someone would come out of nowhere and tell me I couldn't be there.

"She's half Golden Retriever, half Yellow Lab," I said to the attendant, and this time, I asked him, "Can you walk me over to the building and take me inside?"

I am often unsure of what I need. When I first had a white

cane and was not regularly using it, a blind friend said to me one day when I was about to leave for the airport, "Take your cane out as soon as you get there. You'll get more help that way." I had not before thought that I needed more help, or I was leaving it to chance to a greater degree. Maybe I would not need the help, maybe I would. How could I know? I didn't want to be limited. The help makes me conspicuous, but it is also reassuring.

I move through airports as I do through the rest of my life— terribly self-conscious, seeking reassurance and protection for a precarious sense of myself, seeking balance, relying on guidance from others, questioning my needs for assistance even as I assert them, questioning my needs for a dog at the same time as I hold tightly to the harness handle. Never having had much physical assistance before, or never having acknowledged fully enough the assistance I've had, I find it hard to accept my need for it. My self-doubts trouble me far too often. I hope one day to rid myself of them so that I can enjoy my experiences more fully.

When I first began to lose my eyesight, I knew that having impaired vision would be a difficulty. What I did not know was that this experience would turn me inward to such a great extent and simultaneously make me sensitive to public gaze and judgment. The sense of being watched externally causes within me a parallel inner watchfulness and self-judgment. Yet I hope that my instinct for my own movement forward will, in the end, be freeing—like a bursting from a shell, like a walk one early morning when things are still and the air is crisp and I am with my dog, her tail high, her nose forward, her fur glowing golden. I am glad to be out with her, taking in the air, not in an airport, not being looked at and commented upon by people, but, for the moment, caught up in an appreciation for the day, taking pleasure in our movement.

PART 4: I'LL TAKE YOU BACK

Chapter 10

Luminarias

I finally saw luminarias—at night in the dark as we pulled the car into the lot behind where Martha's Black Dog Cafe used to be. I had been to the plaza in the small town of Socorro before, but now it was very dark and my vision was limited in ways I might not be aware of until I actually confronted them, until I got outside and began to walk in the blackness among the small lights.

From the car I saw a row of glowing candles in brown paper bags lining the sidewalks of a narrow street. I was excited. I had not been sure I would be able to see these glowing bags on the ground in the night; their light was muted compared with the brightness of electric Christmas lights. But there were so many, and they were festive; ahead they seemed to dot the park-like plaza, spreading along winding paths, rising on steps and on the gentle slope of a hill. They glowed from side streets in front of illuminated stores surrounding the square plaza. Music wafted from somewhere. People walked about. I was happy.

Hannah and I were on a return trip to New Mexico. Each winter when we have visited in recent years, I try to figure out what is happening to my sight. The stark desert landscape, the vast sweeps, the unfamiliar places, particularly at night, all call attention to my vision in ways I later reflect upon. I hoped this trip, like the one we took two years ago, when Teela was first with me, would be special. At the same time, I feared that either my eyesight would fail me more completely, or the world would somehow fail me and suddenly grow dim—no bright spots, no new adventures, no uplifting experiences or final satisfactions.

That night I spent wandering among the luminarias has become for me much more than a memory of small bags of light glowing beautifully in the darkness and a testament to the transitory nature of my sight. It is a recognition of the art that goes into seeing; a picture, as well, of my inner hesitance, my self-consciousness and self-doubts; a picture of the detailed efforts it takes me to comprehend how to move safely and with assistance; a picture especially of the work required to reconcile how I am looked at by others with how, in turn, I must look at myself; a picture of the thought processes that go into learning to step carefully, and into recognizing what I see and allowing myself to enjoy it.

Life slows down when one is blind. Pictures take time to compose. Small moments assume great importance when new sight is needed. My night among the luminarias marked the beginning of a trip of return and recovery, during which I would confront the many ambiguities of my blindness, seeking new resolutions. On that cool December evening, as the luminarias on a small town plaza beckoned me to come close, challenging me to see them again, and to see them differently, I tried to grasp what I could find in their light.

When Hannah, Teela, and I arrived at the festive plaza, it was not even Christmas yet, two weeks before, but the town was having its celebration. I pointed to what I thought was a parking space as Hannah pulled the car into the dark lot. "That's not a space," she said to me, "but there's one over there." Hannah is always saying things like that, telling me that something I think I recognize is actually something else. She tells me gently, not reprimanding me, but with a kind of guidance, lest I be mistaken and forever have a wrong image in my mind.

She parked and turned off the car engine. I got out and came around to the back door to let Teela out and to put on my gloves and a scarf to keep off the cold. I thought about taking my camera because I wanted to have pictures of the luminarias glowing with their strange delicate brightness, but I decided against it since this was only my first sighting of luminarias on this trip and surely there would be more. As it turned out, this was the best sighting—more candles, close to me, spread around so I could walk among them. There would never again be an opportunity to take this same picture. But I did not know that on this night. I assumed magical displays of lights would be everywhere. It's that way with magic, and with sight; you know you've had it only when it's gone. Now I only have this picture in my mind—a dark background aglow with small square lights and me walking among them, starting and stopping, looking down to take each lantern in—to be sure they were there, to remember them.

Leaving the car, I began to walk forward quickly with Teela to look closely at the first luminaria I saw. Then I started to trip, stumbling on a crack in the sidewalk I had not seen in the dark. "Slow down," Hannah called to me from behind.

As I looked at the candle nestled in sand within the luminaria at my feet and up at the glimmering lights ahead on the plaza, I missed my camera. I thought about going back for it, but I had not yet loaded the film. I also thought it would look strange—a woman wearing glasses, being led by a guide dog, stopping here and there in the dark to look through a lens, taking pictures that might flash, getting down close to the ground to stare into the small bags of light. If I had taken my camera, I would have those pictures I now desire. But I am self-conscious, already feeling enough of a public spectacle. People look at me because I am with a guide dog. I did not want to call further attention to myself.

Later that evening as we walked up close to children singing in the far end of the plaza, I saw a man with a camera taking pictures of his kids. I could be taking pictures too, I thought. His camera in the dark did not look strange. But of course, I was overlooking the fact that if I peered through my camera lens in the night, I would not see much, if anything at all. The camera makes visual images darker, and small, and I am not adept at nighttime photography.

So I am left with images without film, images in my mind, images detailed perhaps all the more precisely because I have no external visual record of them, and perhaps also because I now have less skill with my eyes than with my words. I have grown more desirous of creating my own pictures since I have begun to lose my vision—more intent on keeping my images and more fearful of losing them.

The last time we visited the town of Socorro was a year ago on Christmas Eve. The year before that, I had taken delight in seeing electric Christmas lights while driving around this town, and I had longed to see luminarias—not the plastic kind, but the real ones, usually set out only on Christmas Eve. Hannah had said, "I'll take you to see them next time." And she had. It had snowed last year, so the little bags sat on the plaza in the scattered whiteness of the snow, the ice glinting all around them. They looked picturesque. I was touched that Hannah took me to see them but also disappointed because the candlelit bags looked dim to me, less striking than I had expected. Because the weather was bitter cold last year, I did not stay outside for long walking among the small lanterns. I got back in the car and we drove around the edges of the plaza peering at them. Through the tinted car windows, the luminarias looked even more faded; and farther away, they were harder for me to see.

Hannah then drove us up a road that climbed the side of the mountain behind the plaza, so I could view luminarias lining houses and yards there, and perhaps see them better. She pointed out to me that the mountain in the background was white, and covered with snow, and that above it was a sliver of a moon. But I could not see the snow on the mountain or the moon in the distance, and the luminarias around the homes looked dim there too.

Since I had been disappointed last year, this year I prepared myself. I planned to get as close to the candlelit bags as I could and to give myself many possibilities to see them on our trip. I wanted to take my disappointment and convert it to a satisfaction. Maybe I would light some luminarias of my own or stand close and watch people putting them out in front of their homes. I had called the local Chamber of Commerce to ask if there would be a luminaria display before Christmas, and now, here we were.

AMONG THE LIGHTS

I began to walk quickly forward with Hannah, Teela guiding me toward the excitement ahead on the plaza. We passed lighted store-fronts, warmth emanating from inside them, with pictures hanging on their walls. This night was a combination "arts and crafts crawl" and luminaria display. The stores stayed open late, featuring works of local artists. Walking down the street, we stopped first into a bicycle shop that displayed crafted woodwork and framed photos, with refreshments set out on a table inside. Someone recommended the black bean salsa dip and I had some, a first taste of the red chile flavors I so like. I switched Teela's leash to my left hand so I could reach for a corn chip and sample the smokey flavored dip, which made Teela start to get excited and move around, so I quickly shoved the food in my mouth and switched her back. "Would you like some wine?" Hannah asked. I did but was afraid I would not be able to juggle it well while holding Teela, and what if I got drunk and began to weave on my feet as I walked with her in the dark among the luminarias? I couldn't risk it. I had some more salsa, and we headed back out into the cold. It was not bitter cold like last year, but cold enough to be in the spirit of the season, cold enough to make the shimmering bags of candlelight feel protective—these little fires all around threw a warmth disproportionate to their tiny size.

Hannah stood with me at the curb in front of the bicycle shop before crossing the street to the plaza. "Be careful," she said.

"When we go across, there's going to be construction. There will be a rough area. Can you have Teela follow me?"

I was worried. I could not see the construction. I saw only the glow of the candles across the way in the dark making flickering patterns dance in the part of the plaza nearest me. I shuddered. How could I follow Hannah if I had no idea, if I didn't quite understand what she was talking about? Was the construction in the street or across it? What exactly did it look like? How could I give directions to Teela if I could not see in the dark? And the thing is, that is why I have Teela, and why I need warnings and directions, because I can't see, I can't know all the time what's there. Although I am prepared, I am often unprepared for my lack of sight, as if suddenly, out of nowhere, I will be lost.

I turned to my dog. "Ready," I said to Teela, "follow." We tagged after Hannah, close on her heels. On the other side of the street, I stepped forward. "That's the pile of debris I was telling you about," Hannah stopped me. I still could not see it. "Tell Teela to go around it," Hannah directed. I was thinking that Teela wanted to go forward into the grass on the plaza, to make a beeline straight ahead. Or that was my fear, that she wouldn't lead me properly. I tend not to trust, or not to trust at first. My blindness, my sudden loss of vision, throws me into an immediate state of panic until I gather my senses, figure out what to do—what the direction is, where to step, and exactly at what moment.

I had been thinking, for some time, that navigating outdoors at night on this trip would be good for me. It would be good practice to be plunged into such darkness as I often avoid. I would have to trust Teela more than I must when I am out in familiar places in bright daylight. Back at home, I am often proud to find that I trust her at night more than I did at first—to stop at all the curbs, to take me around parked vehicles, to keep going straight when she should. On this trip, I would often be in unfamiliar territory at night. I would have to follow Teela in the darkness when I did not know where I was. I felt almost giddy with the adventure of it—with the luminarias shining everywhere, the paths among them not clear. I was not certain where the construction lay, where the steps went up, where walkways ended and the grass began. It would be a challenge to find my way through the maze of shimmering lights. I followed Teela cautiously at first, then a little more loosely, more freely.

"You're going off into the grass," Hannah said. "Halt," I told Teela. She was generally good in following paths, but I would have to tell her which direction and be aware of changes in the texture of the ground beneath my steps.

Almost as soon as we began walking, I wanted to stop to look down at the luminarias at my feet. I stood over one bag and then another and looked into the flickering candlelight beneath me. I knelt to get closer; then I turned and aimed my sight at a line of luminarias stretching along a pathway. "Wait," I said to Hannah, "I want to see them." "There will be more," she said.

I now stood and looked around in all directions. The lighted bags were everywhere. How could I take them all in, how remember? The farther luminarias seemed less bright to me than those closer, but I saw them—weaving in patterns on the ground. The bags were brown, but they looked golden. The streets bordering the square plaza had luminarias set out in front of the stores, lining the edges of the sidewalks, defining the perimeter of the plaza, itself crisscrossed with the tiny fires winding along the paths. The plaza looked like a tapestry made of threads of glowing filament, with stitching that stood out in small bunches here and there, igniting the scene with gold in the night.

I wanted my camera. I looked around. How would I ever take a picture of this? I was sure I could, and unsure at the same time. And the picture I was thinking about, was it the image I might take with my camera, if only I had brought it, and if only I could see through the lens, or was it the picture I was now actually seeing with my surveying eyes? That picture was "almost there," I felt. It was almost organized enough, but not quite, for it was marked by the absences and distortions of my impaired vision. Still, I saw the luminarias. There were enough of them to be bright enough for me, and I was close enough to touch them. Instead, though, I looked. I tried to organize the space, the pattern, the picture. That picture is blurrier in my mind now than I want it to be, and the lights in the distance seem so small, as if they are tiny and bright but about to fade away—to get lost in the surrounding darkness. I fear I will lose them forever from my sight, that as time goes on, I won't retain this same picture. It's confusing. I see so much darkness. Yet the small square lights stand out.

As I gazed at the lighted bags on the plaza, I held my right hand up to my right eye and formed a circle with my thumb and forefinger, then looked through it, sighting along a row of the lights, moving the focus from one part of the park to another. I was trying to imitate a camera, to see what I might see if I had brought one, hoping I would see better that way. The camera lens helps define a space, I have found, making a scene memorable. I wanted definition, something composed and bright to stand out clearly forever. Why do those lights in the plaza now look so small in my mind? The whole scene keeps fading. I think they were larger when I saw them, though they were blurry, and even then, receding from my sight, fast becoming a memory.

I stared into the candlelit darkness.

"Where do you want to go next?" Hannah asked me.

We were now standing at the upper end of the plaza near a gazebo where, on a raised platform, children were singing Christmas carols. "Let's listen to the singing," I said. We walked forward and stood close to the stage and listened as the children from an elementary school sang "Rudolph" and "God Rest Ye Merry Gentleman" in small, high, excited voices. Teela perked up her ears, having been remarkably patient during all my stopping to view the luminarias. Then a teacher stepped forward and introduced a new song, made up by one of the children. "Stamp your feet for Chanukah," the small voices began, and I thought about how

Hannah and I were Jewish, standing there surrounded by Christmas and Christianity, and suddenly, just for us, they were singing a Chanukah song. I was grateful because I had been worried that Hannah would feel alienated, and I wanted her to enjoy the event with me. When outnumbered, I tend to forget that I am Jewish, or I remember but become fearful of possible hostility. The singing helped. I smiled, but I still felt an irresolvable contradiction between Christmas and Chanukah—much like the contradiction I sometimes felt between my sight and my blindness. These two very different worlds often seemed to threaten or to negate one another.

IN LIGHTED STOREFRONTS

"Where do you want to go now?" Hannah asked as the singing ended.

"Let's walk over to the stores."

I followed her across the street, stepping carefully over a row of luminarias on the sidewalk after Teela stopped for me at the curb.

"Let's go to the corner store," I said. "Are you sure you want to go there?" Hannah asked. The store seemed inviting to me because its windows shone brightly in the darkness, but it turned out to be a closed real estate office. Next door, a gift shop was open. I followed Hannah into the bright interior, aware that I had to be careful that Teela not bump me into the fragile imports on tables or knock them over with a sweep of her tail as she pulled me quickly through the aisles. I was seeing my surroundings oddly, because I had to look hurriedly at the shelves as we passed them and because I tend to see pieces of things close up best: a belly of a pottery vase loomed large as I sped by, then part of a hanging tin Christmas ornament, a portion of a woven design on a rug. In my disjointed vision, the objects and spaces in the store felt separated from each other and at confusing angles. I asked Hannah to tell me the colors of a Mexican rug I began to handle. "Purple, but cheap-looking," she said. The shop, with all its shapes and colors, felt fascinating, but overwhelming. "Maybe another time, I'll look more closely," I said to Hannah, feeling a small pang of loss as we left.

I followed Hannah through an interior passageway to the store next door, a confection shop, where cookies and drinks were set out on a table. Near the window, a woman displayed handmade silk scarves. Hannah held one up to me as Teela and I began to walk past her. "What color is it?" I asked. It was blue. I did not think I needed a scarf and I wasn't sure about blue, but more importantly, I did not want to call attention to myself by stopping to try it on. Later I wished I had. I rounded an aisle with Teela and heard a customer say to someone, "They have biscochitos here"—the small cinnamon and anise cookies that I like. I bought some, carefully balancing making change, holding Teela's leash, and handling the two bags of treats, feeling I didn't quite have enough hands. Hannah offered to carry my biscochitos, but I wanted to keep them from cracking and to carry them myself, so I put them in my shoulder bag. So often Hannah and I have moments like that, when she offers to help me, but I reject the help, wanting to know I can do a task myself, needing to feel capable.

We stepped outside and back into the cold, then into another building, a financial office of some sort with impressive paintings on the walls—many of them large, bright scenes that I could see. I marveled at them. I stood, with Teela at my side, a dog signifying I am blind, staring at these colorful artworks and wondering what other people saw when they looked at me. Did they wonder why I was standing here taking delight in these pictures if I had a guide dog because I couldn't see? I was thrown back suddenly into my inner place of self-doubt, as if the very brightness of the shop called it forth. I felt less protected here than when I had been outside walking in the plaza in the darkness. There, I could see less, and others could see me less well, but in this bright shop, I could be seen and, I feared, judged.

I stepped over to look at a small painting on a side wall. Then

I walked up to a very large and brightly colored picture of a landscape and stood before it for a longer time. I hoped that people would think it made sense, that I could see this painting because it was big. Then I would not be viewed as seeing too much for a blind person. I felt caught between hiding my vision and wanting to enjoy it, between seeing what I could and wondering what I was missing.

Reluctantly, I left the vibrant paintings and we stepped outside. The next shop was a beauty parlor with a row of empty chairs, huge transparent hair dryer domes on top of each, sitting ready as if waiting for nonexistent customers. Beside the chairs, a mirrored wall reflected an eerie, half-dim nighttime light. Just inside the front doorway, a long table with a bright lamp above it was spread with artful handcrafted pottery—plates, bowls, mugs, goblets, a vase. The potter, a woman, was standing behind the table. On a smaller table to the side, she had set out a large vat of posole. Hannah spooned a bowl of the stew for me. It was warm and tasted wonderfully spicy from the red chile. As I stood sipping it, I hoped Teela would stay calm and not suddenly startle me so that I'd spill it. "Would you like me to hold her for a moment?" Hannah asked. "I can manage," I said instinctively. Then I took her up on her offer, giving her the leash. "Maybe for a minute, so I can look at the pottery."

At the display table, I stood looking down at the bowls and cups, which I liked and wanted to handle. I began touching them to feel the textures and the shapes, but I also hoped I might feel the colors. The outsides of the bowls and the mugs looked black to me, though possibly brown, with tan inside. I asked the potter to describe the colors for me. "They're earth tones," she said. "The outside of the bowl you're holding is brown, the center is a deep rose." I picked up a vase and felt its oval-shaped belly; I picked up a goblet. "That has a brighter rose inside," the potter said. I fingered the central area of a low sculpted serving bowl. "That's almost a purple, it has more blue." I was surprised that I had thought so many of the interior colors were tan. I liked that they were earth tones. I wondered if I had actually seen the rose colors the potter described, or if I only had seen the tans and browns, and imagined the others.

I looked closely at each ceramic piece as she described it to me, straining to see, holding the bowl up to the overhead lamp to try to make the light glint off the glaze so I could see the color. Suddenly, there it was, a shade of rose deep within the bowl, a brighter rose lining the goblet. The exterior glaze that I had thought, at first, was black looked definitely brown in these varying lights. I touched the colors all the more thoughtfully, still trying to feel them.

"Would you like to buy one?" Hannah asked. "No," I said, thinking of the fragility of the pieces and of how I wasn't really fond of rose. Everything seemed fragile—the pottery, like my vision, so fragile and temporary.

We left the pottery in the beauty shop and headed toward the nearby Plaza Bar—on sidewalks lined with luminarias, the crosswalk also lined with the glowing lights. No traffic was allowed tonight on this portion of the narrow street that circled the plaza. I walked beside Hannah, following Teela, taking in the excitement of the night. Luminarias stood at the open door to the bar. Electric Christmas lights hung on the walls inside. We stopped in briefly, but the bar was empty, the night early, the smell of beer lingered in the darkness. As we left, I wondered what lay further inside in the bar's back room. Hannah had taken a quick look, but I never saw it. Yet oddly, that room stays with me as if I had seen it—a dark interior space with tables around a wooden floor beckoning me to enter.

Farther down the street, as we stood at a curb ready to cross to lighted stores on the other side, a horse-drawn carriage began passing by in front of us. "Be careful when we go across," Hannah cautioned me. "There's horseshit in the street." Again, I thought about what I could not see. I didn't know exactly where the horseshit would be so I instructed Teela to follow Hannah's footsteps closely, hoping that the difference between Hannah's steps and mine would not be too great. "Am I okay?" I asked her. "You're doing fine. Step to your left a little. We're almost there."

On the other side of the street, we entered a storefront, formerly a pharmacy but now the local Chamber of Commerce. Amid tables laid with refreshments and Chamber literature, a group of people stood around chatting. Framed paintings, photos, and drawings hung on the walls. These pictures were smaller than those in the financial office. I would have to go up close to the walls to see them, but the tables blocked the way, and the pictures were placed high up, too far for me to make them out. As I pondered what to do, a woman came over and greeted me, saying she recognized me from a previous visit. I wondered if it was me she recognized or Teela. As she began talking, I enviously eyed the walls of inaccessible pictures. "Can you go over and look at them for me?" I asked Hannah later. "Tell me if there's anything you think I would like. Or if you particularly like something, you could describe it to me."

Hannah went up nearer to the walls and looked at the artworks. "They're nice," she said, coming back, "but you're not missing anything." Still, I felt I had missed. Maybe if I had gone up to the walls myself, I kept thinking, there it would be, the perfect picture, my picture—something beautiful and delicate, yet bold enough for me to see, that I could delight in.

"I want to walk around in the lights some more," I said to Hannah as we left the Chamber storefront and crossed back over to the plaza. "Remember the construction," she cautioned. I suddenly stumbled into it, before Teela could stop me. We turned right and walked along a winding path toward a less populated area of the plaza where the walkways seemed wider, rambling off to quieter streets. I looked at the luminarias at my feet and around at the whole scene. I wanted to go down every path, inspect every one of the small lanterns. I did not want to leave without meeting each candlelit bag.

At one point, with a bright street light overhead, I could finally see a pile of the construction debris that Hannah had described to me.

"We're crossing a side street," she said a moment later, "but it's closed off." I was surprised that I had not noticed that we had stepped off the plaza into the side street, that I wasn't able to distinguish a street from a path. Both were surrounded by luminarias.

"It's so pretty," I said to Hannah.

Just then on our stroll, we met some people we knew who had already heard we were in town from the woman in the Chamber of Commerce. "Isn't small town life great!" the man said, welcoming us. I knew I liked to go to small towns. The difference, the change from home, the quietness pleased me. Maybe for a blind person it would be okay to live in a small town, I began thinking. But the transportation could be difficult, people relied more on cars. I knew Hannah worried about that. But I'd always thought I could do it. I could make the adjustments. Blind people live everywhere. People would know me. I would walk with Teela. Then I worried, what if I got bored?

THE ART GALLERY

I stepped up a curb following Teela onto a well-lit brick sidewalk and opened the door of a shop ahead. Music played inside, the strings of a mandolin. This was the town art gallery, lively with people, abuzz with light and sound. Hannah and I had been to a party here two years ago, and that occasion now merged in my mind with this one. I could see somewhat better now than I had last time, when cataracts had made my vision darker and more blurry. Two years ago, I had just come home with Teela, so I was very self-conscious and proud. How should I stand in a gathering with a dog? I had wondered. Should I take off my coat? How did I look? What should I do if people started to pet Teela? I did not want to seem unfriendly. I remember that one man I knew came up to me and put his face close to mine and said, "Susan, it's Peter." I was glad because I would not have recognized him otherwise.

As I looked around now, I had many of these same concerns. Although I saw better than before, my vision remained fuzzy, with pieces missing and dark shadows interfering with the images before me. The glare from the lights overhead blurred my surroundings and I could not focus well enough to keep track of the people moving about. I was relieved that my vision was not perfect, not a night-and-day change from before, for I had become used to my lack of sight. I knew I had to be on my toes and aware. I had to look directly at objects—at people, or parts of people, and parts of the room—to get a sense of seeing them. I could not sweep with my gaze as I imagined I used to back when I had normal sight. I was aware that I had to take extra time to work at seeing in the overwhelming busyness of the gallery. Filling in and compensating for the missing pieces, creating a pleasing portrait, guessing at what objects were—this was my art now, I thought, as I focused on looking about, seeing neither as I had before nor as everyone else did. I was constantly composing—in my mind—the images I saw only partially with my eyes so that they would not seem confused, but would make sense, and so the world would feel hospitable to me.

The glare in the brick-walled gallery was everywhere, jumping off all the surfaces, streaking the air with waves of milky light. I was worried about my blind spots jeopardizing my movements. I stood still so that I would not back into people or bump into the sculptures on display in the middle of the room that I might not see. If I moved, I thought, I would have to gauge whether there was enough room for both Teela and me. I wasn't sure, so I thought I would let other people come up to me. Someone did. A woman who had read my last book came over and said she liked it. That pleased me.

I saw several women standing beside a table next to the front door. They seemed familiar, but I couldn't quite tell. Maybe I had seen them the year of the earlier party. But my vision was not clear then and it wasn't clear now—it was a fuzzy recollection of something that had been even fuzzier. I thought perhaps I should go up and say hello to the women. I had a feeling I was being looked at by them. But I didn't move. I wasn't sure who was who, so I thought I would wait. Blind people always wait, I have told myself many times—as I wait for buses, or a ride, or for something to happen, or to make sure of what I see, or size up a new place. I've told myself, "It's normal. Blind people wait more." I have found that thought helps me be patient. At an event like this gallery open house, it was reassuring for me to feel that waiting was okay. I did not have to go directly up to people and be social.

I also did not go up to the walls and look at the pictures, which surprised me. Here I was in an art gallery and I wasn't looking at the art. I assumed people would understand, thinking I could not see well enough. But I did not go up to the pictures, in part, because the gallery, though beautiful with all its colorful art, felt like both an obstacle course and a fishbowl. There was no direct path among the sculptures. I would have to make my way with Teela in narrow spaces, possibly bumping into people, or knocking them with the bag that hung from my back with the biscochitos puffing it out. I would then have to put my face up close to the pictures, and someone would come and ask what I was doing.

Not wanting the attention, instead I stood. I put my hand out toward a black metal sculpture near me to touch it, but then I drew my hand back, afraid the metal could have sharp edges and I'd cut myself. I told Teela to sit. I felt less alone here with her. Hannah was off looking at the paintings in an adjoining room. I thought it might look better if I touched some of the sculptures, but still I did not. Then I noticed the musicians getting ready to play. That would be nice, I thought, folk or bluegrass music. It did not involve moving or seeing. It would take the focus away from me, and Hannah would like it.

Hannah was invited upstairs to see the studios of several of the artists. The main artist, a woman we had met before, said there was a spiral staircase going up to a loft area. I knew I would be unsure of my steps on a spiral staircase with Teela, my limited sight, and my height fright, so I declined. I walked over to a shelf near the front door and picked up a brightly colored guide to art galleries in the area. Maybe Hannah and I would use it later in our travels. I could take out my lighted magnifier and look at the colored pictures in it.

I slipped the guidebook into my bag, then Teela and I stepped back into the center of the room and stood beside a huge horse. The horse, a sculpture, was almost life-sized, about the size of a pony, and painted with soft-toned rainbow colors. Its back was arched, its tail up, its head thrown to the side in abandon. I knew this horse from our visit here before and it felt like an old friend. I stood in the middle of the room beside it, surrounded by smaller sculptures on pedestals, and behind them by the paintings on the walls. To the side of the room, where the musicians stood, were tables with refreshments. I wanted a drink, but I didn't move. Someone offered me wine but I declined, thinking if I wanted it, I should get it myself, wishing not to sacrifice a sense of my own competence in this wonderful yet confusing space, thinking, too, what would I do if while I was holding my glass, Teela started to bolt?

I felt lost in my surroundings now, in the brightness of the room, which made artworks and people blur together. Outside, the luminarias stood out individually in the darkness and seemed more defined. I yearned for the comfort of that lesser light.

The artist who had painted the horse came downstairs with Hannah. I knew that she and her partner were lesbians, and I wondered how many other lesbians were here, and if the other artists whose work Hannah had seen upstairs were lesbian. Probably not, I thought. A woman standing by the doorway looked familiar to me; I hoped she was a lesbian, but she looked straight. They all did, although perhaps I could not see the subtle clues that would lead me to make a distinction—the presence or lack of makeup, the way a woman smiled, a direct look to her eyes. Still, I would see the big clues, I thought, such as a defiant stance or a very butch haircut. At the party here two years ago, there had been a small group of lesbians present, women whom I knew were lesbian because we had been introduced in a friend's home earlier. But I would not have known by looking, and it was not necessarily because of my eyesight. This was a place where the women looked straight. I probably looked like a lesbian, though I wasn't sure. I felt like a statue standing here in the middle of the art—a statue of a lesbian, blind but with glasses, accompanied by a golden dog, self-conscious, smiling occasionally. I hoped that if I smiled, it would disarm all objections.

I was nervous now, and tired from standing. This open house was not as exciting as the more intimate party had been that last time. But it was a check-in for me, an occasion that caused me to ask, who am I now, and how am I going to deal with it? I felt poised as if on the verge of an answer.

We left the art gallery that evening, stepping outside, Hannah and I intent on our privacy, and we talked about who, if anyone, was a lesbian, how people were doing, what the pictures were like, and where we might go for dinner. As we walked back over to the plaza, I was glad to see it was still lit with the many luminarias. I was reminded of how the year before when we came here, I actually took a few pictures. I am still not sure how I saw through the camera, but the flash went off and I took them. One, in particular, has great meaning for me. I must have been standing below an overhead lamp or very close to the luminaria to see through the lens, so what I have is a photo of a luminaria seen close up; in the background is snow on the ground, a bare mesquite bush, and a bench. The flash has gone off, so it's not a picture of a golden glow in the dark, but of the entire bag reflecting the light of the flash and the candle glinting within. The outlines are amazingly clear when I put the photo under my magnifier. The bright bag is toward the center of the picture. I see it in my mind better than what I actually saw that night, perhaps because I was busy trying to take pictures with a camera, or maybe I didn't see that luminaria as well in person as when I looked at it in the photo later.

I was glad that tonight, the milder weather meant I could walk among the luminarias for a longer time, step slowly, and look down and see them. Perhaps because I had been disappointed last year, and because this time I prepared myself for dim lights, all that I had seen tonight felt like a gain—a brightness I had not expected would be so bright, the lights so plentiful. There seemed to be more luminarias on the plaza this year, definitely more on the streets surrounding it sending forth a glow, and they were ringed with art—with bright pictures and weavings in the stores. And the buzz of people looking at the displays lent a legitimacy to my focus on my own sight.

I felt exquisitely aware as I moved around in the darkness of the plaza looking at the glowing bags of light, and then curious as I came out into each brightened storefront. It was a special night. I did not have my camera, but I kept trying to take pictures: of the chairs in the beauty shop sitting empty in the night with their plastic domes on top, waiting for the next drying job, for the invisible people who would arrive the next day when the beauty shop certainly would be open, though gone would be the pottery and the red chile posole, gone as swiftly as my walk around the plaza. I wanted to hold onto my sense of what it had been like, to hear again the children singing, taste the black bean salsa dip, feel the colors on the pottery, step carefully, once more, over invisible horseshit. I looked into the darkness and yearned to stay longer.

This has been a story of some of the lights I saw on a small town plaza one night, never perhaps to see them quite the same way again. I have tried to create the pictures I did not take with my camera. This picture in words of how it felt and what I saw—as I moved between darkness and light, seeking self-acceptance, and trying to keep images from fading from my view—this memory of a dazzling array of glowing paper bags shining more brightly in the night than I ever expected reminds me of my desire to enjoy both the fleeting moments of light and the longer nighttime darkness. Especially, this memory of my night among the luminarias represents a gift from Hannah—a gift of patience, of taking me back, of braving Christmas and giving guidance and instruction, asking where I want to go next. I am often so lost in a sense of my own separateness, increased now by my blindness, that I forget that I am not alone. I am sharing the path, the adventure, the meandering walk, holding a leather leash and grasping a harness, Teela in front of me, Hannah by my side. It takes three of us now. Teela led as we headed up the sidewalk lined with luminarias, walking toward the parking lot back to the car.

Chapter 11

Heading South

The next day, we headed south. That day appears very bright in my mind. Unlike the night before, it was basked in sunlight and blue sky. Our journey was full of changes in place and cautions for me about my vision. Looking into broad expanses of rolling plains dotted with green cactus and brush, I marveled at the landscape—broad enough for me to see, cool in winter, endless, unpopulated in the areas where we drove.

That morning, we stopped at a state park where a dammed-up lake lay ahead. "I'm not sure about driving farther," Hannah said suddenly. This road goes straight into the water."

Looking toward the lake, I was convinced her fears were needless. I didn't understand. It was only after Hannah parked the car and I got out that I saw that, indeed, the corrugated pavement led directly into the water, with no wall or fence marking the edge—where it served as a boat ramp. I suddenly felt fearful because of the danger I now saw, but I also felt relieved. My loss of vision was real, as marked in the bright sunlight as it had been in the dark night, although more hidden in the daytime because the colorful, dramatic desert scenery around me seemed so tangible that it was hard to remember I was not fully sighted. Ahead, the shapes of huge brown mountains backed the mirrorlike blue lake.

We drove deeper into the park to an area where I wanted to see cactus. As we approached it, I asked Hannah, "Where are the cactus?"

"All around you," she said. "Look straight ahead."

But I could not see any cactus. I saw only rock walls lining the edge of the parking area, gray stones stacked on top of one another. Hannah pulled the car close to the walls, until finally I saw not gray rocks, but massive dark green and aged pear cactus sitting solemnly in the sun. I could have walked right into them without knowing. My eyes play such tricks on me—tricks that both delight and terrify.

We drove farther south, stopping for lunch in Hatch, a dusty chile-growing town amidst fertile fields near the Rio Grande, where small shops by the roadside displayed hanging red chile ristras. The dried red chiles made the air smell pungent and musty. In an intimate Mexican restaurant, I sat next to a warm cast iron stove and ordered a chile relleno, eager for the taste of green chile and cheese. Teela lay comfortably under the table while Hannah and I talked about our plans. When I went to pay for our lunch, I stood at the register and handed the waitress a bill. "Here's a 20," I said. She took it, then handed it back to me moments later. "You gave me a 50," she said. "You've got to be more careful." She paused, shook her head, then added, "Not everyone will be as honest as I am."

I took back my $50 and quickly gave her a $20 bill instead, feeling patronized but pleased to be recognized as blind. I also felt a wave of cold shock because I had overlooked something, made this mistake. It wasn't a life or death matter, but it carried a sense of "what if"—what if this hadn't been only a paper bill, what if it was something bigger—what if my life depended on my not making a mistake and I just didn't see, but instead assumed, going along almost unconsciously by habit? What if I was not aware enough and something terrible happened? I felt more shock and fear than I had when mistaking the cactus or the road to the lake.

After lunch, Hannah and I walked down the main street in Hatch toward a corner crosswalk to reach a store on the other side. I went ahead, following Teela, then stopped at the curb and waited for Hannah. I knew she liked to be in charge of our street crossings in unfamiliar places, for she worries that I may get hurt. Yet we each cross streets differently. Hannah watches the cars and looks at the faces of the drivers, establishing eye contact. When she has negotiated that the driver will give her the right of way, she feels it is safe to cross.

I used to do that, but because I no longer see the faces of the drivers, or even that there is a driver in a car, I stand and wait at intersections. Sometimes I wait only very briefly, then I signal to Teela to go forward and we step down off the curb quickly and cross. I first listen until I have determined that it is safe, either because the traffic has stopped or because there is no traffic, or I wait until I hear that an approaching car has slowed because it sees me. I rely on drivers seeing me, because I cannot see them. And I rely on stepping off the curb and moving to the other side quickly after I have signaled, doing it in one smooth motion to make clear to drivers that I am going and in what direction. If I hesitate, drivers may assume that I am giving them the right of way and I could be hit.

Hannah and I clearly have opposite approaches. She hesitates at curbs just when I am about to stride forward. My sense of safety comes from being seen, hers from seeing into the eyes of others. When we are together, I almost always defer to her style, although I think I have gradually taught her to realize that when I step to the curb and execute my signals and motions, the traffic treats me as a blind person by stopping and waiting. Sometimes it is less confusing to cross the street my way.

At the corner in Hatch, I turned to Hannah. The street we were about to cross was a section of the highway that cut through the town, and the traffic was coming fast. "I'll follow you," I said to Hannah. "Tell me when it's safe to go."

"Now," she said.

"Forward," I told Teela, raising my right arm near her head and pointing forward. Now I was crossing the street my way, like a blind woman, eyes straight ahead, ears listening; Hannah was doing it her way, looking toward the traffic and the eyes of the drivers. I glanced to my right as I crossed and noticed that a car had stopped near us, and I wondered what the driver saw. Could the driver possibly be aware of our orchestration, the subtle mixing of Hannah's and my ways of crossing a street, the slight tension between us, my hesitation at the curb on the other side while Teela stopped to show me we had reached it—the fact that all of us were so very concerned for my safety?

Once across the street, we entered a variety store to look for a blanket for Teela to lie on in the car. On the way back, we actually crossed the street mid-block, which I knew a blind person should not do alone. But Hannah was with me. She stepped forward, looked to both sides, gave me a signal; I put my right hand on her back this time, touching her left shoulder, walking behind her while heeling Teela at my side. This was "sighted guide" style. I began to run. "Slow down," Hannah said. "No one's going to hit you."

We left Hatch, driving out past the chile fields, the farmland soon giving way to vast expanses of arid, straw-colored desert. Railroad tracks ran beside the road, the sun glaring down as the radio played country and western songs. An occasional Border Patrol car zoomed by. Above distant mountains, a blue sky held high white clouds. I had a sense that we were on our way to new possibilities as the sun lowered, signaling the lateness of the day. Finally, we turned onto a side road that curved, then began to climb up toward gentle mountains, entering the Mimbres Valley. In place of a barren landscape, trees now loomed alongside the road and lined the nearby narrow river, their bare branches reflecting the golden setting sun, the fields behind them the color of winter wheat. The Mimbres River Valley was more picturesque in a conventional sense than the open desert, but of a piece with it. And I was becoming used to the contrasts, to going from a vastness to a sense of close detail, much as with my vision, I move in and out of seeing—sometimes getting a broad view, blurry, with parts unrecognizable, at other times focusing closely in, yet finding comfort in each vision, supplementing the one with the other.

Darkness had settled by the time we arrived at our bed and breakfast in the woods. The innkeepers led us to a mobile home nestled among trees on a hillside on their property. I had requested this mobile home for privacy, and it seemed just what I had wanted—a rustic woodsided trailer set apart from the main house. To enter the front door of the home, however, meant navigating a small flight of steps with no banister. I faltered. I could not see the wooden steps in the darkness and I worried about how I would maintain my balance when carrying our luggage up them. The innkeepers generously offered to bring the bags, and although I was grateful, I felt useless and incompetent, embarrassed because I was afraid of the stairs.

The next morning, I practiced on those steps, going up and down them without looking, counting them, touching the side of the mobile home to keep my balance. Next time I wanted to be able to carry the bags myself.

Later that first night we drove to dinner in a neighboring town. I tried to give Hannah directions but got us lost on the back roads. Much that I did now was more complex than it used to be. The roads were not where I expected them on the dark map in my mind. "There it is," Hannah said finally, finding the turn. I soon saw the fuzzy shape of the restaurant—what looked like a house with a lighted front porch. Hannah parked across the street from it. As I stepped out of the car, I feared the darkness and the cold, unsure how I would reach the restaurant across the way.

"Wait for me," Hannah called.

I stopped beside the car with Teela, wondering, should I take Hannah's arm or go forward without her into the darkness?

I listened and heard quiet. "I'll be okay," I told Hannah. "Forward," I instructed Teela and we stepped out into the pitch black night, nothing visible but faint lights on the house across the road. The darkness was imposing but exciting. I felt like an explorer braving the unknown. Once across the street, Teela and I quickly climbed the several stairs to the porch, where white Christmas lights hung above the front door. I felt pleased to have made my way across the dark street and up the steps without tripping. Hannah soon arrived and stood by my side in the glowing white light. "You made it," she said, sharing with me this small moment of conquering my fears.

After dinner, back at the mobile home, I asked Hannah to come with me when I took Teela outside to relieve herself. The ground near the mobile home was sloping and rocky and I was still unfamiliar with the wooden stairs. I knew I could have taken Teela myself, but I wanted Hannah's reassurance, her company.

The next morning when I went out to take a walk with Teela alone, I found myself uncertain of my steps through the brush and dry leaves in nearby fields, even in the brightness of the day, so I came back soon after setting out. Later, Hannah, Teela, and I walked together in the woods on paths covered with dry fallen pine needles that softened our steps and looked like snow, reflecting sunlight from clouds above. That day had a gentle golden feel. Our time in the Mimbres Valley was special—several days of walking in the woods, nights in the mobile home with a piñon fire and a warm bed. "We're very lucky," Hannah said. For me, time had stopped. I could not see, but I felt protected here.

I ate the biscochitos each morning for breakfast, heating them in the oven, filling the home with their cinnamon and anise scent. My blindness made me more limited in my mobility than I wanted to be. I could not drive by myself to find flat places where I could safely walk, and I could no longer navigate on the irregular hilly terrain and in the dry rocky stream beds and arroyos as I used to do. Now the stream beds and arroyos stretched before me as roads untaken. Yet the frustrations did not destroy my sense of well-being. And the comfort I viewed in the landscape was, in part, because my blindness lent a softness to the scenery, blending the trees and fields together. Sometimes I yearned for clarity, for the individual tree shapes to stand out, but I also accepted the softness as a gift of my blindness.

The day before we left the Mimbres Valley, we stopped at the small Mimbres General Store, where I had an experience that stays with me like little else. The store was jam-packed with hunting and picnic supplies and tourist items. As I stood at a glass counter looking at a tray of turquoise and silver earrings, Hannah pointed to a pair she thought I might like. The woman behind the counter reached beneath the glass, searching with her fingers for the pair Hannah indicated, but she could not find them. A younger woman, coming over to help, quickly reached in and lifted out the earrings and handed them to me. I held them up close to my eyes. Then I took out my lighted pocket magnifier. "I don't see very well," I told the women. "So I have to hold things close. She helps me," I gestured toward Hannah.

"I don't see either," the older woman said quietly. She seemed to me to be in her seventies and she was wearing glasses. It had not occurred to me that she couldn't see.

I asked if she had a magnifier. She shook her head. I handed her mine to try. She held it close to a page and seemed pleased with what she saw. Handing it back to me, she soon came out from behind the counter and told me, with a tone of sadness, that she had macular degeneration.

I lifted my arm and pressed the button on my talking watch to cheer her by having it announce the time. She lifted her arm and pressed the button on her talking watch, a smaller version of mine, both from Radio Shack. She smiled broadly.

"Do you have a white cane?" I asked her.

"No," she said. "I pray. I don't give up." She told me that she lived in a house behind the store and could walk to work. She had lived there for seventeen years. Her vision had only deteriorated seriously five years ago. She had an operation, but then it got worse.

"Maybe someday they'll find something for me," she said. "I won't give up praying."

It took me a while to grasp her meaning. I had thought that not giving up meant you still did things, you got the aids you needed. But for her, not giving up meant you still prayed. You did not lose faith.

"I don't drive anymore," she said, in a questioning manner.

"I don't either," I said, as if this were our bond.

I reached into my backpack for one of the black felt pens I always carry. "For you," I handed it to her. "It writes a thick line that's easy to see."

She went back behind the counter while Hannah and I browsed further in the store. I kept wanting to go out to the car and bring in the white cane that I kept there as a backup and give it to her. I was not a believer in religion, in reversals of eye conditions that don't reverse, in waiting for cures that might come someday. I had to restrain myself from going out to get the cane.

"She doesn't need it," Hannah whispered.

I went up to the counter to pay for my items. When the older woman gave them to me in a bag, she also handed me a ballpoint pen with "Mimbres Store" written on the barrel.

As we drove away from the store, I wished to return, to give her my cane and to talk some more. In my mind, I see her to this day making that walk from the house to the store, reaching under the glass counter for things she cannot see. I see her as more helpless than I am, which is not necessarily true. I need rides. I reach for things I can't find. In the Mimbres Store, I bought a hunter's cap and a pair of earrings that I do not wear because out of their environment and in brighter light, they don't look very good on me. In my desk drawer, I keep the pen that the woman in the store gave me. I don't use it because it writes too fine a line for me to see. But it helps me remember. I had wanted my encounter with the woman in the store to seem friendly and my attempts to be helpful to have meaning, for such acts of sharing give a purpose to my blindness.

Driving south, this emotional moment behind me, I thought of a stop by the roadside, a chance meeting, two strangers who hardly knew each other, and yet we did.

Chapter 12

Back to Big Hatchet

I remember the view as we approached Big Hatchet. We were driving south through the broad desert surrounded by a bright blue sky when I saw that just ahead near Big Hatchet, billowing white clouds had gathered, and over the peak of the mountain, a dark cloud hovered. As we drove closer, Big Hatchet loomed larger in front of us while the tower of majestic fluffy clouds tumbled around it, the sunlight glinting off them. It was as if an invisible force above was playing in the sky, dramatically setting forth these glowing shapes, singular in the vast, flat desert. I expected thundering music from overhead, a sudden shaft of golden light, and a deep voice announcing that on this day, the Goddess made the heavens and earth and left this mountain here for me.

More mundanely, I looked ahead at the familiar silhouette of Big Hatchet, the wide range and the hulking dome and peak I so liked. I watched the black cloud above it and worried. Had I come all this way to find the top of my mountain blocked from my view?

"Clouds move," Hannah said, seeking to be reassuring. "By the time we get there, it will be clear. You'll see your mountain."

We turned at the intersection to the small town of Hachita, the nearest to Big Hatchet—that windswept group of buildings by the road across from an abandoned railroad track bed. We had planned to stop at the Hachita Store.

"It looks closed," Hannah said as she pulled up to it. I got out and looked into the broad store window and, indeed, the black shelves inside were empty, the lottery and game machines gone. No little Mexican figurines or bright green and pink ashtrays were on sale, as they had been when we visited here two years ago. A couple of tables sat by the front window, but no sugar or salt shakers rested on them, no fresh pot of coffee stood on the counter. Some of this I saw, and some I just thought about as I stared into the dark empty space imagining what was no longer there. On the right side of the store, where shelves had once held cans of Sterno, matches, paper towels, and soap, and where a woman behind the counter had cordially told us it was five miles to Old Hachita and advised us to take Route 9 through to Columbus and then to Mexico, no one now stood. The emptiness was haunting—a worn wood floor, an interior as desolate as the desert outside, yet, at the same time, full of an imaginary life.

I was sad that the Hachita Store was closed. Like so much else in my life since I began to lose my eyesight, this place seemed to have passed me by, disappeared before I could figure out exactly how to remember it. Still there was something about the closing that I found comforting. I rather liked going to places no longer there, that people had left.

Hannah now stood beside me, reading a sign taped to the door of the closed Hachita Store. "It says there will be a meeting on Wednesday night at the community center," she said. "Though I'm not sure where that is, or what year this sign was put up."

As we walked back to the car, I noticed that the gas pumps that used to be in front of the store were gone. Or maybe they were there and I just didn't see them, since my peripheral vision has blind spots. I looked around and they seemed gone. Definitely no ponchos with big horses on them blew in the wind out in front as they had that first time we came here.

Next door, the Hachita Cafe was also closed, quietly gone out of business. Farther down the road, I looked for the boarded-up brown building on stilts, the Hachita Tavern I remembered from before, but I couldn't find it.

We turned south, driving for the last ten miles on a straight, lone asphalt road leading nowhere farther but to Mexico, until we reached the turnoff—a hardly noticeable gap beside the main road, where a dirt road branches off heading closer to Big Hatchet.

We turned at the gap and drove in past familiar brownish-green cactus and the brittle bush and creosote that I remembered fondly from our earlier visits. Two years ago, I first came to Big Hatchet. Last year, Hannah had taken me back, knowing how much I wished to see it again, to feel it not beyond my reach or sight, not suddenly inaccessible, and we drove nearer to the mountain. Now we were here once more, as if this dry seemingly barren place was a kind of wellspring. Big Hatchet loomed black and large out my side window. I remembered how glad I had been the first time I saw it, and I was happy again now, and more relaxed. Although my vision was brighter now than two years before—not as much brown murkiness stood between me and my mountain—my sight had not changed all that much. The surrounding mountain ranges and the cactus looked extremely small to me, thinner, and more blurry than they should. The desert surfaces shimmered as if under water. I lifted my binoculars to see Big Hatchet better, to see details, to see something like what Hannah saw with her naked eye. The clouds were dancing above the mountaintop, the large dark cloud still hovering.

Hannah drove toward Big Hatchet with determination, grasping the steering wheel, going fast. The first time we visited, we had been timid on this dirt road, Hannah hesitant to go far because she did not have a map; I was afraid because I wasn't driving and thus did not feel in control. I kept expecting us to get caught in sand traps or ruts. On our second visit, Hannah drove us even farther, turning in on a road that led directly toward the mountain. Now she seemed determined to take me right up to it. I felt touched. Her taking me here was a testament to our desires to continue our adventures together despite my loss of sight; it was evidence of Hannah's generosity toward me.

As we turned and drove in closer to the mountain, the rutted dirt road suddenly dipped down. A bathtub sat beside it—an empty cattle watering trough. There was dampness in the air. In a nearby field, dry yellow grasses bent, blowing in the wind. This stretch of land looked different, not bare and dotted with prickly cactus and starved brown bushes, but smooth-looking, the grasses waving, welcoming us.

We drove farther until the road turned east, hugging the base of the mountain along its undulating, long, dark north side. Big Hatchet felt very close to me now. I took up my binoculars. I saw three peaks separated by deep ravines. What I had thought was the "dome" of the mountain was actually an overlap of two of these peaks, an illusion created from afar. I thought about how often what I see turns out to be something else.

We parked the car at a junction with a rocky path that led up a slope on the lower portion of the mountainside. We'd go for a walk. I took Teela out of the car to let her relieve, then hooked her up in her harness. I put my camera and binoculars around my neck—gestures that had been new to me two years ago, but that I now had become used to, readying all these aids for my sight before I ever took a step. The air was bright and it felt exciting to be here. It was late afternoon and I was standing amidst cactus and mesquite taller than I was, Teela by my side eager to go, Hannah waiting. We began to climb up the slope, passing century plants with towering candelabra flower stalks fuzzy to my eyesight but large enough for me to see, past soaptree yucca, and tough prickly pear cactus, past another cattle trough. The ground was rocky. Teela led me and I followed her, careful about my footing and my balance. Hannah walked ahead of us and called back to alert me to places where small cactus grew in the roadbed so I could direct Teela around them. I did not want my faithful guide getting prickers in her paws. She wasn't bred a desert dog.

Scattered cattle roamed these arid fields, I knew, though none were visible and the land seemed hardly nourishing enough for them. The large dark cloud above Big Hatchet remained, but lighter in color. A windmill stood ahead of me on the rocky slope, looking wooden and small compared with the dark mountain backdrop, but picturesque, a destination for our climb. As we neared it, I saw a deteriorating square cement enclosure that must have once held water for the cows. It was quiet up here above the plains but for the wind, and the dust, and rocks and a lone ocotillo. We climbed farther as if we could, with our tiny steps, climb all the way up Big Hatchet.

"I think you can see the main peak now," Hannah said. I looked up and there it was. The dark cloud had brightened enough for me to make out the mountaintop.

As I stared toward the several peaks and the cloud, everything around me looked black and white. The mountain was dark and the air white from the light clouds overhead, and it was that time of day when the world often looks black and white—like an old movie or a simpler time. If we were to get stuck out here, I thought, it would be a long time before anyone came and found us, before a rancher or a migrant worker happened by. Maybe we'd have to spend the night, curled up in a canyon, nestled in soft leaves in a safe place on the side of my mountain. Somewhere up there, there had to be a refuge.

I stood now and looked out on the surrounding plains. I put my arm around Hannah and gave her a kiss. I was happy to be here.

"I'd like to take a picture of you," she said a bit later. Then she posed it with me in front of the windmill, the sun on my face, Teela close at my feet, a tall ocotillo plant with its spiny arms raised nearby, because she knew I liked ocotillo. I have saved that picture. Hannah bemoans the fact that the windmill and the ocotillo are smaller in it than she planned. But for me, the photo says I was there, with her.

As we came down from our climb, I turned and looked back toward Big Hatchet. The windmill stood with the dark mountain behind it, the gray cloud overhead, and I snapped the shot. Hannah likes that photo because the windmill is centered between two peaks as if embraced and the picture seems composed. In my mind, I keep trying to detach the windmill from the picture, to see a smaller portion of the whole. I try to enlarge it, as I am accustomed to doing with my binoculars and my reading magnifiers. My sense of what reality looks like has changed. I now go for the close-up.

Back at the car, Teela drank water and I inspected the soles of my boots. They were all torn up. I had been stepping directly on the sharp edges of rocks as we climbed the slope. I had been so intent on keeping my balance while following Teela and looking up at the mountain and the cloud that I had not been fully aware of where my feet stepped. Under any other circumstances, I would have been dismayed that my shoes were destroyed, but because Big Hatchet did it, I felt strangely calm.

I became sad as we started to drive back, the mountain diminishing outside my window. I asked Hannah to stop at a place on the road where she and I had ventured the very first time we came here. From that spot surrounded by desert, I looked out at Big Hatchet, trying to recapture my first view and hold onto it. We stopped again where the dirt road from alongside Big Hatchet begins to merge into the paved asphalt road that heads to Mexico or back up to Hachita.

"Do you want to go farther south?" Hannah asked, as if sensing my wish, "and see what it looks like?"

"Yes," I replied.

We turned and drove straight for several miles, then rounded a bend where the sun shone brightly. Suddenly, the view changed. No longer was there the long silhouette of a dark mountain, but something brighter, reflecting the sunlight. Big Hatchet looked more rugged from here, and rounder, more a pointed shape than a long stretching mass with a peak and dome at one end. It looked like a sky island in the literal sense of a triangle jutting up from a stretch of flat land, as an island might from the sea, a place in the midst of no place. The face of the mountain looked stony, like craggy rock cliffs pasted on top of one another; parts of it looked green, perhaps from the deep canyons. The sight was impressive, but this was not *my* view of Big Hatchet. It seemed to be someone else's mountain now. It was not the hulking shape I had learned to recognize from a distance as I scanned the skies whenever we drove in the south. It looked small to me. Was my vision diminishing the mountain's size, or was it the changed angle of view?

I soon noticed that there were now no clouds in the sky above the mountaintop. I wondered if the large, hovering, dark cloud was still over there on my side of Big Hatchet. But the sky seemed totally clear. It was odd, I thought. The mountain was clearer from this view but had less character, less drama than on the darker side with the threatening clouds. Perhaps I liked that darker side even more now because I had learned to value my own darker vision, to appreciate the drama in simple black and white shapes, to feel at home with the landscapes I saw through my blindness.

I glanced over at Hannah, who was also contemplating the mountain, and thinking, most likely, about the lateness of the day. We decided to turn back, maybe because another time we'd go farther, or because it wasn't in our plan and the new area felt strange. But we left with reluctance. As we drove north toward Hachita, we passed a turnoff—another dirt road that led toward the mountain, with what looked like a trailer parked at the end of it. "Maybe next time we can go there," I said to Hannah.

The sun was now very low in the sky, throwing a sparkling light on the roadside cactus and on the white-tan earth and the scrubby bushes, and on the shape of Big Hatchet, smaller and more hazy behind us as we drove through the glistening desert plains.

I reached down and touched the torn sole of my right boot. I had this reminder. Teela sat up on her seat in back. The surrounding landscape was slipping by me all too quickly. The only consolation I had was that perhaps I'd be back. It seemed almost unbelievable to me that Hannah and I had been here three times, coming all the way out here to visit a mountain.

I don't know why I go where I do, perhaps to compensate for some deficiency—my loss of eyesight, my fears of getting lost in the lives of others. Perhaps simply because I like remote places. What I do know is that I was sad to leave Big Hatchet and I hoped to return, and that meanwhile, I would keep an image of my mountain so that I could revisit it in my fantasies. Strange that I'd seek comfort and haven near a mountain so far away when the real comfort was always closer to me—in my inner ability to find pleasure in my travels, and in my relationship with Hannah—in her arms, her willingness to make me happy. Dramatic clouds had signaled my coming to Big Hatchet today. Far less dramatic was the quiet affection we shared, less easy to see than a mountain, but no less there.

Chapter 13

The Hachita Bar

With the sun now about to set, we pulled into the town of Hachita, turning left on the road that parallels the old railroad track bed where empty stores faced the desert fields across the way. Driving past a row of dark abandoned buildings, we stopped in front of a white building with a sign over the door that read, "Hachita Bar." I had not seen this bar on our trip here two years ago when we had parked beside the boarded-up brown building on stilts, the Hachita Tavern of my memory. That day as we ate our lunch in its shadow looking out toward Big Hatchet, I had imagined coming back and going inside the tavern later, meeting people, and staying in the boarding house upstairs overnight. But we had left Hachita without ever stopping in, and when we returned to the town last year, we could not find the boarded-up building, nor had I seen it this year.

Instead, what stood where the weathered tavern should have been was this spiffy white-painted Hachita Bar with a black wrought iron door in front. On our last visit, Hannah and I had noticed that on the right side of the building, an artist had painted cartoon figures of a miner with a handlebar mustache and a flat-fronted prospector's hat, a scantily dressed woman chasing after him, and a cow's skull below, along with lettering that said, "Hachita Liquor Saloon." Hannah took pictures of the cartoon figures and of the front of the white building. I had often looked at them and wondered what became of my weathered brown tavern.

Tonight as we pulled up, a car and a pickup sat in front of the white Hachita Bar. Seeing lights inside and the door ajar, I wanted to go in. Maybe they would know where the other Hachita bar was and why the cafe and the store were closed. I knew that the cigarette smoke in bars bothered Hannah, and we had much driving yet to do, but she agreed to stop in. I was looking forward to a drink.

It was dusk as I opened the front door and stepped inside cautiously behind Teela. Hannah followed me. Although it looked blurred, I could make out that a polished wooden bar ran along the right-hand side of the narrow room, extending back, stools pulled up next to it. A pool table stood in the rear, its green felt glowing under bright lights; up front, the lighting was subdued. A bartender in a white shirt stood behind the wooden counter, polishing glasses, liquor bottles on a shelf behind him.

"Hello," he said.

"Hi there," I offered in my most friendly and casual-sounding voice.

It was a long time since I had been in a bar. Bars, for me, have always been lesbian places, where I have gone, especially when alone and before Hannah, to socialize and be part of a group. I never minded the cigarette smoke or the ambiance. I liked the "other world" feeling, the sense of a forbidden night life. Once in Albuquerque when I first knew Hannah, I took her to the bars I used to frequent and we danced the New Mexico two-step. Another time, we went line dancing, or she did, at a bar hidden behind stores without any sign outside indicating its presence. But here in Hachita, there was a sign and a bartender. We were lesbian; but the bar was not. I had a guide dog and it was becoming night.

As I stepped into the darkened interior, I reached my hand in front of me to feel for a stool, took it, and sat down. Hannah pulled up a chair next to me. I told Teela to lie at my feet. To my left, a woman patron sat engaged in conversation with the bartender.

"Howdy," she said. A man sitting a few seats back from her seemed to be the only other customer.

"What'll you have?" the bartender came over and asked me, still polishing the liquor glasses, a towel in his hand.

"Do you have red wine?" I asked.

"Burgundy," he said.

The woman beside me seemed to smile. "That's what I'm drinking," she offered.

"I'll have that too," I said, relieved not to have to decide further what to order.

Hannah asked for a ginger ale and for directions to the restroom. While she was gone, I pulled my stool closer to the woman next to me and we began to talk. Teela served as the ice breaker. "She's a nice looking dog," the woman, named Flora, remarked. "I once had a Lab," she continued, and then she started to tell me about herself. "I do the insides of the buildings over in Playas," she said.

The bartender soon brought me a white paper cup of water and put it down on the bar. I was waiting for my drink, and when it didn't come a few minutes later, I asked after it.

"I gave it to you," the bartender gestured. "It's right there in front of you."

I lifted the paper cup then and found that what I had assumed was my water was red wine on ice. I thought I had seen the light of a refrigerator door opening down at the other end of the bar. Flora, too, I noticed, had a paper cup in front of her, though she had a glass as well. I sipped my chilled Burgundy, thinking that this was a woman's drink here, and there probably was not much call for red wine, or for white wine either; probably it was mostly beer. The smell of the red wine on ice reminded me of being in college and of a time when the red wine was either Burgundy or Chianti.

Hannah returned from the restroom. I introduced her to Flora, explaining how Flora had been telling me she worked in Playas. The bartender had deserted us and was now down at the other end of the bar talking with the male patron.

I wasn't sure exactly what Flora did inside the buildings, so I asked her.

"I tear them out and remodel," she said. "I put up sheet rock. I hire people, but I do most of the work myself."

I was impressed and surprised. She did not look like a construction worker. She seemed to me small and pretty, about my age, maybe a bit younger. Her voice was throaty, like that of a woman who drank and might have smoked and was older than her years. The bar was darkish, but light enough for me to see the general contours of her face as she leaned close to mine.

"They keep blowing up Playas," she continued, sipping from her paper cup. "It's the military. They have a lot of remodeling to get the houses ready for the people who come down. The houses were falling apart. Playas used to be a town, you know. But they kicked the people out. It's a military base now."

"I heard about that," I said. "With the metal fences?"

"Yeah. It's closed to the public."

She didn't sound pro-military, I thought, just reflective and chatty, as if this was a curiosity of life. I imagined her tearing down walls in the homes and putting up sheet rock.

"The people who work there, most of them only come down for certain months. When they're gone, it's very quiet," Flora said. "I kind of miss the explosions."

I knew that the U.S. government was using Playas to test emergency procedures in the event of a terrorist attack. Although not far from here, the town seemed distant because it lay on the other side of the Little Hatchet mountain range, to the south and farther west than Big Hatchet. It hurt me, what the government was doing to my part of the country. Here where the land stretched toward Mexico and where I hoped to find my solitude and individuality, they were blowing up buildings and converting a town to a military base.

"I live in Hachita," Flora continued. "I moved away, but now I'm back. People don't stay in Hachita."

I thought a minute about how I wanted to stay and make Hachita my home, ignore the military playing games in Playas, live close to Big Hatchet.

Flora ordered another paper cup of wine. I sipped from mine as the ice cubes melted. The drink felt refreshing now that I was used to it.

I told Flora a little about Hannah and me, that we were from San Francisco and we were teachers. It seemed better, I thought, not to be nameless and unidentified, to feel more connected—people knowing where you came from, a bit of who you are. A bar was a public place, I reminded myself. We were all passing through, all travelers here for this moment in life. I didn't want to feel too much like an outsider, an intruder, too much as if I did not belong. I imagined it could have been me putting up walls in the houses in Playas or working for Flora, that, but for the chance of fortune, or how I was raised—Jewish and bookish and intended for intellectual work—there I would be. I felt a wave of sadness that because of my upbringing and my ambitions, I could not actually be on a work crew down in Playas or anywhere in that part of the desert. I couldn't quite fit where some of my dreams led me. But that didn't stop me from imagining them as if they were real, as if I could live here. I'd get a ride, because I couldn't drive a truck. Teela would come with me to the work site. I'd watch. There would be something for a blind woman to do.

Hannah, who had been listening, now leaned over the bar and asked Flora and the bartender, who was standing near us, about Hachita. "We noticed things were closed," she said. "What happened to the cafe and the store?"

Flora answered, "Maria closed the cafe a couple of months ago. She's going to beauty school in Arizona. It's what she wanted. She's in Phoenix now."

I remembered we had met Maria that first time we passed through here. I had walked inside to look around and bought some muffins from her. We had also met the owner of the Hachita Store, who had given us directions to Old Hachita.

"And the store?" Hannah asked.

"Jean still lives in Separ," Flora said. "She ran it on her own for a while. But then she closed it. There's not enough business around here."

"Was there another bar?" I took a deep breath and addressed the bartender.

"Nope," he said. "This is the only bar. Oldest building in town. It was a bar once before, then not, then a bar again. My father bought it in 1972. I took it over from him. I'm John Starkey. He was James Starkey. Been here since 1972."

"It's a nice bar," I said.

I looked around. While I had been talking with Flora, I had been glancing across the way to a room behind where John Starkey stood, past the liquor bottles on the shelf beside him. That room had chairs and tables in it. I now asked Hannah if she had seen it when she went to the restroom, since I had been wondering exactly how to get to it. "It's a mirror," she said gently. "The tables are behind you." I swiveled in my chair and, surprisingly, there they were. In the low light of the bar, I could easily make this mistake, for mirrored images often look real to me. Still I was taken aback because, thinking I see, I forget that my vision is not reliable.

I asked Hannah for directions to the restroom, got up with Teela, and walked to the area in front that she mentioned. After searching for a long time in an alcove, I still couldn't find the restroom. I felt along the walls of the square alcove with my hands, touching the wood paneling, trying to locate a door. I must have felt along the surfaces of the walls twice. At one point, I was ready to cry because I was so blind, and the day had been long, and Big Hatchet and even this bar in Hachita would soon be behind me. Finally, I found a doorknob, but it led only to a broom closet, and another seemed to lead outside. Then my fingers grazed the metal of a very small latch that opened the door to the hidden restroom, which, unmarked, had seemed part of the larger wall. I felt embarrassed that it had taken me so long to find it.

"I told you," Hannah said when I returned. "You should have let me come with you."

We stayed in the Hachita Bar a while longer, until I finished my chilled wine. The bar was not physically very warm, but it was bright and cozy compared with the outside, and people were willing to talk. I felt taken in, warmed by the hospitality. It does not require much—a friendly word, a drink, a sharing of experiences, a restroom. I put down my money for our bill after Hannah read me the amount, and we got up to go.

"Did you see the wall?" Flora asked as we stood. "The painting was done by our local artist." She pointed to the wall behind the tables and chairs. Hannah walked over and looked at it; there were cartoon figures on the wall like those we had seen outside. I looked but saw only the suggestion of scrawled black lines, so Hannah told me about the images and admired them for the two of us.

We exchanged parting pleasantries with Flora. "Good luck with the remodeling," I said. "And take care with your health." She had told me of her problems.

"Good luck to both you women," she said. "Enjoy the rest of your trip."

John Starkey wished us safe traveling. "Thanks for stopping in," he said. "Come back again."

I stepped outside, following Teela into the cold night. Back in the car, sitting talking with Hannah, I hardly believed I had been inside the Hachita Bar. It wasn't the bar of my memory, the tavern I had expected to enter and yearned to enter. I wasn't sure that bar ever existed—the boarded-up brown building on stilts. Yet it must have. Maybe they tore it down—Hannah suggested that explanation for why we couldn't find it. But with so many deserted buildings around here, it seemed unlikely. Out here, they abandoned buildings and left them to crumble by themselves. There was no need to tear them down. No one needed the space. You could just build farther down the street.

I was beginning to feel that I had to accept that as far as the rest of the world was concerned, this was "the" Hachita Bar, the only one located just about right here. It was a different bar than mine. In my bar, Hannah and I had spent the night two years ago. My bar was a figment of what I saw then, of what I could see and what I couldn't, and what I could remember. It was rather peculiar. No one had ever really been there.

"Which one do you think was the real Hachita Bar?" I asked Hannah. "And where do you think the other bar went, the one that was all boarded up?"

"I think they tore it down," she said.

"Or maybe we just didn't see it," I offered. "Maybe I remembered it wrong."

We drove on into the darkness past fields almost invisible except for occasional glimpses of cactus and barbed wire fence posts catching pieces of the car headlights. The road, though bumpy in places, was flat and not too rough. Teela lay on the back seat sleeping, having done her work for the day, taking me up and down a mountainside, in and out of a bar, to places that I hoped she would remember. Would I ever again return to Hachita, and to Big Hatchet? I wondered. Would I ever return to Hachita again after dark, late enough for the bar to be open? Would Flora keep tearing down inner walls, keep doing most of the work herself? Would someone else buy the Hachita Store and restock it and open it; would they ever again have ponchos outside with horses on them blowing in the wind, as I saw that first time? Would they blow up Playas completely and then abandon it, letting it settle into the desert dust? Would we come back and see the south side of Big Hatchet, that other view that did not feel quite mine? Would the Hachita Cafe with the big sign on the side that said "Home Cooking" ever serve really good food?

Would I ever *not* want to return here? I wondered. I doubted that last possibility. I would do it in my sleep. I would do it in my blindness. I'd remember—a bartender in a white shirt, a mountain, a trip with Hannah.

"Thank you for taking me," I said to Hannah and reached over to stroke her hair. "We made it. You took me back."

"I told you I would," she said.

"Would you have stopped in that bar if you weren't with me?" I asked her.

"No. But I'm glad I did."

Chapter 14

Traveling Blind

We drove north, mostly in silence, each of us thinking, listening to the road. I was glad to be with Hannah out in this strange nowhere, trucks soon breezing by on the interstate. We stopped in Lordsburg and had dinner at Kranberry's Family Restaurant, where we had stopped two years ago for a takeout lunch. Back then, when we drove east to Big Hatchet for the first time, I had not known how wonderfully resonant that destination would turn out to be—how much the mountain would become a beacon for my sight, a place to reflect on, return to, look at and wonder—what had changed, what was important? Not only the mountain served as this kind of marker, but so, too, did the road approaching it, the towns and stops along the way, the nature of my intimacies with Hannah and Teela, the surprising revelations of my blindness no less than of my sight.

We now drove up to Silver City for the night but returned to Lordsburg a few days later to explore the town. I have this fondness for abandoned places. Like Hachita, but larger, Lordsburg was a town passed by time, a gray cluster of buildings in the dusty southern desert dotted near and afar with peaks of sky islands. It was a railroad, mining, and ranching community with stores empty but for leftover goods and odd pieces of furniture that no one seemed to want to take away. Walking with Hannah and Teela down the main street, I stared into store windows that I had only gazed at from the car as we sped by in search of gas and lunch on our earlier visit. Now I looked more closely into the abandoned storefronts and could see the blurred shape of a naked mannequin wearing a bridal veil, as if half dressed for a wedding, a collection of dusty, old, colored bottles, stacks of used magazines, brown empty space. We ate lunch at the Junction Cafe across from the railroad, where I stared at a deer's head over a door, listened for the rumbling of freight trains, and talked with Hannah while Teela lay quietly under the table.

That morning, we had driven to a scenic area, Red Rock, where I watched a deer eating a yellow cactus fruit and caught a glimpse of a roadrunner—not unusual animals for a desert river canyon, but for me, it was all unusual. I saw the deer and the road-runner by using my binoculars and the telephoto lens of my camera, with Hannah directing me where to look. Seeing the images come into view pleased me. Even more, Hannah's patience in guiding my eyes moved me, as it had so often on this trip.

After lunch, we drove farther down the main street of Lords-burg alongside the railroad tracks. I looked for the gas station where I had asked for a tire gauge and an air pump two years ago and they'd had one but not the other. That gas station was now boarded up, gone out of business like so much else around here. Farther down the road, we stopped at the intriguing Hot Winds Rock Shop, where Styrofoam cups stuck in the holes of a cyclone fence beside the parking lot spelled out "Merry Christmas," the round, white bottoms of the cups creating the design. At night, I thought, the cups would reflect car headlights; this was a poor person's luminaria display, another kind of Christmas light, reflect-ing a drier, more remote place where things come and go quickly but Styrofoam lasts.

Inside the rock shop, I peered at the sliced-open polished rocks as Hannah pointed out interesting patterns to me. I was surprised that I could not fully see the colors and details in the striated stones. Here in this hard, dry land, they collected rocks as I do images, I thought; the lines in the stones were wavy, the colors subtle—tans, grays, purples. I lifted a heavy dinner plate made of stone and a heavy bowl—the true desert pottery—and I remembered the earthenware I had handled on the festive Socorro plaza not long ago, when I had walked among the luminarias, similarly straining to see.

In the back of the Hot Winds Rock Shop were clothes, not the tourist kind, but heavy denim pants, flannel shirts, jackets, big belts, cowboy hats—clothes for the railroad men, I imagined, who had spilled something on their pants or needed a change. I so often imagined such scenes, both because of gaps in my vision and because of my propensity for fantasy. My imaginary world seemed so very real, the line between conjured and actual more blurred since my loss of sight. How much, on this trip, had I actually seen? How much did I invent? I prized my ability to be creative, but always I wanted to see what was truly there—to have Hannah describe it to me, to touch it, explore it, hold an object up to the light, magnify and study it until I got a sense of the whole, an image that was partly visual, partly not—made up, as well, of touch, feel, and understanding.

Next on this route of our return, we visited the local Lordsburg Museum, housed in a large domed armory building with a cannon and a towering windmill out front. Inside were displays of army uniforms, vintage housewares, historic town photos, and a striking educational diorama depicting a Japanese internment camp that was here during World War II. Clearly, in Lordsburg, there was more than meets the eye, reminding me of that other mystery—that I must always search for what lies beneath what I see, for what is invisible, or perhaps lost in a blind spot. I asked in the museum about Big Hatchet. "Our boys used to go hunting there," the woman in charge told me. I was grateful that she had opened the museum today just for us, driving over in the winds of an oncoming storm. I was searching for further information.

"Do you know of any books about the mountain?" I inquired.

"I read Louis L'Amour. He has things out there." She lifted a well-worn paperback she was reading. "Not this one, but you might try *Shalako*."

I made a mental note to find it, perhaps in audio format, and see if I could bathe in his words about Big Hatchet. I knew Louis L'Amour wrote western potboilers, but I wasn't being choosy.

A few nights later, Hannah, Teela, and I arrived in Albuquerque where I suddenly began to cry while carrying our luggage up the irregular and worn wooden steps to our lodging. I did not trust my footing or trust Teela to guide me, and I missed the country and Big Hatchet. I swore I would never again stay where I did not know the steps, arrive in the night, and nearly fall. My fear was undermining my sense of equanimity, of being able to go places with ease. It was unsettling a self-confidence I did not even know I had found near Big Hatchet, with Hannah driving, the vistas broad, my steps often on flat ground, except for the rocks, those sharp rocks that had torn up my boots on the mountainside.

On the ride here through vast stretches of desert in the dark, I had felt safe in the protective cocoon of the car, Teela's faint dog smell in back making it homey, Hannah close beside me. We were nearing the end of our journey, but it felt like we were starting out anew together, the moon a bright orange sphere rising over a distant mountain—splendid, as if placed there just for us. Now, though, I cried, totally miserable as I came out to the car repeated times for our bags. Hannah and our host offered to help me, but I wanted to do it myself. Distressed as I was, and afraid for my footing, I knew there were only a few steps and I needed to know I could manage, as if bringing in our luggage helped me make peace with a new place.

The next morning in the sunlight, I went out and stared at the several troublesome steps that had unnerved me. I put my head down low to look closely at them. I climbed up and down them practicing, as I had taught myself to do when challenged, and as I had done often on this trip. The practicing reassured me that I would be all right, no obstacle would become too limiting.

That night, we attended a party with friends. On the drive there, Teela sat on the floor at my feet while I looked out the car window at Christmas lights and electric luminarias that pierced the nighttime darkness. These glowing lights reminded me of the many gifts of my lack of sight. They stood out in a simple, beautiful relief and made me happy. Although they were small and merely dotted the darkness, they were large in my mind, clear by contrast with the background, reminding me less of what I could not see than of what I could, glowing with memories of other lights and other places.

When we arrived at the house where the party was being held, I could discern a few candlelit luminarias in paper bags placed along a front walkway. Several other luminarias seemed to be hanging in midair, though they were actually overhead on a wall I could not see. Teela led me briskly toward the front door, Hannah ahead of us. As I entered a darkened interior, I felt a quick step down. In this old adobe home, small rooms opened onto one another, with shallow steps connecting the rooms that had been added on. Steps like these always surprise my footing, so I knew I would have to be careful. I walked forward toward a bright living room wondering, as I approached, was there a step, would I trip, would Teela stop me in time?

Three rooms back, in the dining room, I was introduced to people whose faces I could not make out, but who seemed friendly. I held Teela close, for with food on tables at dog height, she might sneak a taste without my knowing. I felt her pull slightly and I sensed that her nose was twitching, but she was well trained and stayed close. Some of the guests did not realize I had a dog with me, since Teela was low, hidden by the center table and by the density of people in the small space.

One of our friends, Jim, older and gentlemanly, led me

through the house to a back bedroom so I could put down our coats and bags. He offered to deposit them to spare me the trip, knowing of my cautiousness in unfamiliar places, but I wanted to take them there myself. I wanted to know exactly where I had left my coat and bag in case I needed them later if I wished to leave suddenly, or if there was an earthquake or an emergency.

On the way to the bedroom, following Jim, Teela pulled me toward a side wall of a narrow hallway. I had to draw her tightly to me. On the way back, she pulled again, so strongly that it was hard for me to keep her close. Then I realized that in a cage on my left, a small animal was burrowing under a blanket—perhaps a hamster or a gerbil. Teela is a Retriever. I held her leash more tightly and told her "Forward," imagining an overturned cage, a freed rodent, and a chase, and not wanting to be embarrassed by having to corral a disobedient guide dog in a small house full of people I did not know.

In the dining room, Hannah came to my aid. She offered to help me take food. "What do you see?" I asked her, looking around quizzically at the many serving plates. Our hosts, I had been told, prepared unusual foods, which made me cautious, in addition to the fact that I could not see the foods well enough to identify them.

"I think that's the smoked elk," Hannah said.

"I'll pass…" I said.

"I think you'll like this one." Hannah lifted something, probably cheesy. I began to pick up a plate and fill it. Then I stopped. I'd fill the plate and then I would not have a hand free for Teela in case she found another caged animal, or if I needed to pull her toward me to make her inconspicuous, or if I wanted to reach my hand out to stop someone from trying to pet her. What if I needed to make a quick escape or hold a drink? Often on our travels, I had such thoughts. Each new place, each new experience or possibility for eating, was also a time to consider Teela. What does she feel? Is she hungry too? Would she want to take off for somewhere else before I did? My thoughts about her easily supplanted and, by now, were inextricably mixed with my thoughts about my own needs, my mobility, my sight.

"I'll go sit down with Teela," I said to Hannah, looking toward a side room. "Can you put some food on a plate for me when you're finished with yours?"

"Would you like some wine too?" Hannah asked.

"That would be nice." I had long ago learned to let Hannah help me with food in strange places. It seemed easier for me to accept this aid than physical help with steps and bags. The food was somehow more intimate, more part of "us," less about me and the world.

I sat down in the adjoining room and talked with Jim, his wife Marjorie, and a few other people, feeling less alone because I had Teela with me. She lay at my feet, a source of conversation more often than I liked, but I had some formalities I could repeat—phrases about her upbringing and training as a guide dog that I could offer—and I could smile.

Hannah brought my plate. Jim handed me a glass of wine. I didn't quite recognize the food on my plate, and I dropped some of it as I lifted it to taste. I talked with Marjorie about how we were each social misfits, and eventually it was time to leave.

As I stepped out from the warm home with Teela, I was aware that I was moving from the low lighting in the house to what felt like almost total darkness outdoors, but for the few luminarias and a string of Christmas lights overhead on the wall. I walked forward guided by Teela, who followed Hannah as she proceeded on a curving front path. The curve confused me. I wasn't sure of my direction, although Hannah, ahead of me, and Jim, behind me, seemed confident of theirs. I should have trusted following in Hannah and Teela's footsteps, but I did not just then. I wanted my own confidence, even at night in this strange place.

The flagstone path wove to the left, then right, then under something, probably the wall; it turned left again, then in a few more steps, we stopped. Jim went to get the car. Hannah seemed to have disappeared as well. I began to walk forward quickly with Teela. "I'll go with you," I called to Hannah. Then a light came straight toward me. I jumped back, pulling Teela with me, unsure where I was and afraid a car would hit us.

"It's all right," Hannah said, suddenly by my side, "You're on the sidewalk. One more step and you'll be in the street though."

I was shocked and confused. No one had told me I was on the sidewalk. A door opened abruptly toward me. "Step back. Jim is opening the car door for you," Hannah said.

"Where's the street?" I asked her.

"It's on your right."

In that moment before the car stopped, I had been so scared—when I saw only the bright lights, when I did not know where I was. I wish I had asked. I wish I had gotten my bearings before I walked forward from the house onto the path. I wish I had stopped and asked Hannah or Jim, "Where am I now? Where am I going? Can you describe where the street is? Tell me, where am I going to end up? What kind of surface am I now standing on? What kind of surface will that be? Is there enough room for Teela?"

These are all questions I constantly ask myself, but when I have some degree of sight, I can answer them. I can look ahead or assess ahead, I can prepare both Teela and me for what is coming, decide on our route. But in the totally unfamiliar darkness, I can't do that. I can't just step forward unprepared. And that is what I was doing. I can step forward that way, but it is frightening, especially when there are cars or crevices where I might trip, or other possible dangers to my footing. The nighttime darkness held such great lessons for me—about my movements and my awareness and lack of it. This trip had been full of nighttime lessons as well as daytime ones. My orientation was repeatedly in question, my planning, my enjoyment; my sheer terror at the loss of my sight was less frequent than it once had been, but it remained with me. And although the darkness at night raised my fears, I was also discovering that there was incredible beauty in the dark and in the shadowy in-between—the place where both light and sight may fail.

The last night of our trip was Christmas Eve. We had left Albuquerque and were staying farther south near Socorro, where I had seen the many luminarias on the plaza our first night. I had planned that we would drive to the plaza again on Christmas Eve and see the luminarias one last time before we left. But when we reached the plaza tonight, the area was dark, no lights to be seen. The vast display with thousands of glowing bags filled with candles, so vibrant two weeks ago, was gone.

"Don't worry," Hannah said, "I'll find you some more."

We had started the evening by driving on back roads in the small farming town where we were staying. In the gray light of dusk, I had seen a woman lighting a row of candles in bags atop her front wall. The shining bags looked magical to me. I could see their shapes, and the wall, as well as the candlelight because we were not yet in total darkness. Farther down the street, a man was walking, placing his bags along the roadside, then stooping to light them, the line of glistening luminarias standing like sentinels in the night, guarding the road, making it available to my sight.

As we drove on, a more complete darkness began to descend. We passed a house with many luminarias placed at different levels: on the ground, on the front wall, and on stairs leading up to the house. They glowed bright gold in contrast to the surrounding black night. I asked Hannah to stop the car so I could get out and step close to them. I took my camera, desiring a picture, but I could not see much through the lens. My picture, when it finally came out, was blurry—showing three fuzzy luminarias and one off-center on the bottom. I had caught an image, though not quite the one I wished.

We drove farther, past a fiery red tree, its bare branches draped with red Christmas lights. Although artificial, the crimson tree looked beautiful to me. The night promised to be exciting, but when we arrived at the dark plaza, I suddenly felt disappointed by the quiet emptiness. Where were my many lights—the weaving patterns of the candles glinting along the paths, my joy in seeing them? Looking out the car window, I thought that this darkness, too, had a message—a way of suggesting the temporalness, the importance of grasping each moment, enjoying it.

We headed over to the old mission church. There, luminarias lined the front courtyard and the surrounding adobe walls, but bright spotlights overhead marred my sense of the contrast between the lanterns and the dark night. We drove past nearby small homes where people had placed luminarias on porches and in driveways, lights that seemed dim to me. Hannah stopped in front of one house where a woman was holding a long stick, using it to light her bags. "Do you want to get out and ask her if you can watch?" Hannah asked me.

"I don't think so," I said, not wanting to be conspicuous, to look as if I didn't live here, to seem as if I did not take this all for granted, to have to explain—"I want to get close and look over your shoulder because I don't see very well. My dog's name is Teela. She's a guide dog. That's Hannah over there in the car. We're from California." So I never asked. Instead, I looked out the car window and saw only a shadowy figure of a woman holding a wand above dim bags. Yet that shadowy figure haunts me with a simple elegance, more vivid in my mind than if I had seen it better.

We drove higher up to a hilly area of town and found a street with house after house showing luminarias in front, but the lights felt dim and far away from me.

"I can take us up the side of the mountain," Hannah offered. "They had good lights there last year."

"No," I said. I was afraid we would fall off the side of the mountain and worried that I would be disappointed. It was hard for me to separate the sadness that welled up within me because the lights looked dim from my sadness because this was the last night of our trip. I kept thinking I was content, that I had seen enough lights, I did not need to see more.

So Hannah turned the car around and we headed back. As we drove through the dark streets of the town, Hannah stopped for me, when I asked, in front of an old adobe wall that stood by the roadside. She pulled the car close so I could see a row of luminarias adorning the gently arching wall like jewels in a crown, a shining halo above a wooden doorway. I wanted this aesthetic image, this lone display of lights, to fill me with a missing glow. Watching them, I felt like a small lost girl with limited sight having to be taken around by someone else in the dark, not knowing quite where I should be or who I was. I felt a tenderness toward Hannah, and I wanted to cry. I had looked forward to this night so much, to the final luminaria display on our trip. I had expected to take pictures, to see through the camera lens, and all my pictures would come out beautifully.

Perhaps because the luminarias looked dim and blurry, I felt my losses diffusely—the loss of all the places I had visited, of everything I was leaving behind, the loss of my eyesight, my excitements, my wished-for imagery. Though often comfortable with my blindness, I still wanted to hold onto sharpness, everywhere, on all occasions, in every kind of light. I wanted to be able to drive, to see clearly, to be dazzled more than once, to perceive my surroundings in visual terms, to enjoy all the details.

We drove back to our bed and breakfast where I drank some wine and soon slept. The next morning, I woke before sunrise and went out to take a walk, fresh for the new day. I carried my camera, my binoculars, and my white cane. I left Teela in the room with Hannah because I anticipated making frequent stops to look through my lenses and I did not want her becoming cold from standing still. The early morning air outside felt chilly, only the first touch of light in the gray sky. I started walking, tapping the gravel in the driveway with my cane; it quickly got stuck. I knew why I preferred Teela. I found the edge of the road in front of me and turned right.

Across the street, I looked up to see a house silhouetted

against the dark sky. Beneath the pointed roofline hung a string of white Christmas lights still on from the night before, a necklace of softly shining pearls marking the line between the house and the sky. To my eyes, the sight was beautiful. The lights glowed, bestowing a sense of my own special world that had been missing the night before. It was not every morning I could wake and see Christmas lights, and when I'd had few expectations beyond hopes for a colorful sunrise and a private walk.

I continued along an irrigation ditch with a vista of farm fields in the distance. As I walked, I passed houses nestled in shadows, and bare trees resembling dark sculptures against the sky. I heard the rustle of dry cottonwood leaves at my feet. I took a picture of a gnarled tree trunk, aware of the shapes of fences and distant hills and railroad tracks and homes that I could not see with any detail, yet their gray forms and their sleepiness took my breath away. Behind one bare tree, a hint of orange began to color the sky.

I heard a rooster crow. A dog barked. I kept walking. I used my cane. It got stuck. I lifted it. I tried to remember to probe the ground with it as I spun around on the path beside the irrigation ditch, looking at the dark trees with the changing orange light behind them, and at the fields. I didn't want to step too close to the irrigation ditch and fall in or to trip on a tumbleweed. I reminded myself that Teela was not with me. I'd have to do all the work myself. Next time, I would bring her; I'd make sure she stayed warm. This cool and cloudy morning began to feel healing for me.

As I walked back, I turned onto another side road to explore further. A dark house soon appeared in front of me under trees, its edges outlined with bright, multicolored Christmas lights. The image filled me with joy. I took off my gloves and aimed my camera. I would take a picture of these lights to remember this quiet, dark Christmas morning.

When I got home, however, I found that the camera did not capture what I saw—simply colored Christmas lights gently defining a dark home—but instead, it showed a fairly well lit house draped with a few small lights, surrounded by cars in the driveway and pieces of power cords, a trash can, and a fence. What had seemed dark to me in the background of my picture was, in fact, full of detail as far as the camera was concerned. It reminded me of the drama in what I do see. Perhaps more often than I know, I see less than what is there, and thus more. I see images more dramatically, in stark relief, more as a matter of black and white or dark and light, as forms with only some detail. But the details I do see can make an ordinary world magical.

Now it was time to go home. Where was home? I wondered. I wanted it to be here in the desert, in a place other than where I lived in the city; I wanted it to be on the road with Hannah and Teela, in our adventures, in my fascination with the light and the desert vegetation, the shapes of cactus and agave, and the patterns of luminarias. I wanted my home to be where my sight was, my appreciation—and I don't mean only my eyesight—where I found comfort and enjoyment.

I walked back to the house to wake Hannah and greet Teela. We would have breakfast and then be on our way. I'd have to pack the car. There would be goodbyes. I hoped Teela had not missed me too much. I hoped Hannah would take me back here again, and to Big Hatchet and Hachita and to see more luminarias, and to see the morning and evening light, and that she would continue to guide me in the darkness. I hoped to remember to get my bearings, always, wherever I was, to make the darkness less frightening than it might be. I needed to hone my skills with my movements, with my dog, and my cane, with my use of my hands to feel, my use of my words to ask questions. I needed to use my imagination to make sense of it all. I took Teela outside and glanced up into the sky, brightening now before my eyes. Inside, I bent over the bed and gave Hannah a kiss to wake her up. "Did you have a good time?" she asked.

"Yes, I did."

And in my mind we were back in that hot mineral pool in

Truth or Consequences swimming in the green shimmering water, and we were driving along on a dusty road getting nearer and nearer to Big Hatchet, and sleeping in our mobile home in the Mimbres Valley, and wandering among luminarias on the town plaza. Hannah and me—we were bumming around, helping each other, taking each other places neither of us would have gone alone. Teela added to our happiness and sense of possibilities, taking me on new roads, providing me with comfort and safety. I knew I often questioned my sight, wondering whether I had too much of it or too little, but I was getting used to the wandering, the exploring, the constant adaptation, to looking out on the world in which I traveled, getting used to my own individuality within it.

I had Teela by my side. I opened the back of the car and took out the floppy Frisbee that she loved to play with. I tossed it to her and she ran off out of my sight, gleeful, full of a Retriever's joy, and brought it back to me to throw again and again and again.

Maybe somewhere I would find a book about Big Hatchet, I thought, and I'd bring it back and Hannah would read it to me, sitting up one night at home in our bed.

I saw myself taking that challenging sunlit morning walk on the streets of Truth or Consequences with Teela, counting the street crossings, trying to decipher what was in the store windows, the two of us standing peering in. I saw Hannah and me crossing the street together in Hatch, each doing it our own way, working out our signals, then crossing, two women and a guide dog, my wondering what the world saw.

For me, there are no clear dividing lines, no strict black and white, no real goodbyes, no final losses, only many connections, memories, overlaps of light and dark. There are pictures that shimmer and fade, and mountains that linger.

I turn to take a picture of what I've just seen and then it's gone, replaced by another. I have come a long way from where I started out, fully sighted and walking alone. I have seen pieces of my vision slip away. I have had to learn to be careful of all my movements, to stumble on steps and pick myself up and try again, to take pleasure in Christmas lights, to ask for a disabled room. I have had to learn that when I cross borders and experience fear, I can recover. I now memorize maps and places where there are cracks in sidewalks. I need space at my feet for my dog. I won't be helpless and I don't drive. I like mountains and remote places and early morning light. I like the shadows and the darkness more than I ever did before. I see more than my eyes can comprehend. I see and yet I must always remember that I don't see, which is a much harder recognition. I am comprehending the world anew each time I set out. I am traveling blind.

Bibliographic Notes

Traveling Blind uses a personal ethnographic approach developed in my previous studies: *Things No Longer There: A Memoir of Losing Sight and Finding Vision* (Madison: University of Wisconsin Press, 2005), *The Family Silver: Essays on Relationships among Women* (Berkeley and Los Angeles: University of California Press, 1996), *Social Science and the Self: Personal Essays on an Art Form* (New Brunswick, N.J.: Rutgers University Press, 1991), *The Mirror Dance: Identity in a Women's Community* (Philadelphia: Temple University Press, 1983), and *Hip Capitalism* (Beverly Hills, Calif.: Sage, 1979).

There is a limited but valuable literature on relationships with guide dogs and other service animals. Important recent discussions of blind individuals' relationships with guide dogs that I have found extremely helpful appear in: Beth Finke, *Long Time, No See* (Champaign: University of Illinois Press, 2003); and Rod Michalko, *The Two-in-One: Walking with Smokie, Walking with Blindness* (Philadelphia: Temple University Press, 1998). Notable overviews of experiences with a variety of service dogs can be found in: Marcie Davis, Melissa Bunnell, and Betty White, *Working Like Dogs: The Service Dog Guidebook* (Crawford, Colo.: Alpine Publications, 2007); Ed Eames and Toni Eames, *Partners in Independence: A Success Story of Dogs and the Disabled* (Mechanicsburg,

Pa.: Barkleigh Productions, Inc., 2004); Patty Dobbs Gross, *The Golden Bridge: Selecting and Training Assistance Dogs for Children with Social, Emotional, and Educational Challenges* (Lafayette, Ind.: Purdue University Press, 2005); Martha Hoffman, *Lend Me an Ear: The Temperament, Selection, and Training of the Hearing Dog* (Wilsonville, Ore.: Doral Publishing, 1999); and Alison Hornsby, *Helping Hounds* (Surrey, U.K.: Ringpress Books, 2000). Among the popular accounts, three guide dog classics are: Bill Irwin and David McCasland, *Blind Courage: A 2,000 Mile Journey of Faith* (Harpers Ferry, W. Va.: Appalachian Trail Conference, 1991); Patricia Burlin Kennedy and Robert Christie, *Through Otis's Eyes: Lessons Learned from a Guide Dog Puppy* (New York: Howell Book House, 1997); and Betty White and Tom Sullivan, *The Leading Lady: Dinah's Story* (New York: Bantam, 1992). A recent informative "puppy raising" novel is: Elizabeth Wrenn, *Around the Next Corner* (New York: New American Library, 2006).

Philosophic issues concerning the human-animal bond are discussed in: Donna J. Haraway, *When Species Meet* (Minneapolis: University of Minnesota Press, 2007) and *The Companion Species Manifesto: Dogs, People, and Significant Otherness* (Chicago: Prickly Paradigm Press, 2003); and Cary Wolfe, ed., *Zoontologies: The Question of the Animal* (Minnesota: University of Minnesota Press, 2003). See also: Josephine Donovan and Carol Adams, eds., *The Feminist Care Tradition in Animal Ethics* (New York: Columbia University Press, 2007).

Important works on disabled women's experiences that provide context for *Traveling Blind* include: Victoria A. Brownworth and Susan Raffo, eds., *Restricted Access: Lesbians on Disability* (Seattle, Wash.: Seal Press, 1999); Susan K. Cahn, "Come Out, Come Out Whatever You've Got! or, Still Crazy after All These Years," *Feminist Studies* 29:1 (2003): 7-18; Nell Casey, ed., *Unholy Ghosts: Writers on Depression* (New York: Morrow, 2001); Eli Clare, *Exile and Pride: Disability, Queerness, and Liberation* (Cambridge, Mass.: South End Press, 1999); Diane Driedger and Michelle Owen, eds., *Dissonant Disabilities: Women With Chronic Illness Theorize Their Lives* (Toronto, Ontario: Canadian Scholars' Press, 2008); Mary Felstiner, *Out of Joint: A Private and Public Story of Arthritis* (Lincoln: University of Nebraska Press, 2005); Michelle Fine and Adrienne Asch, eds., *Women with Disabilities: Essays in Psychology, Culture, and Politics* (Philadelphia: Temple University Press, 1988); Gelya Frank, *Venus on Wheels: Two Decades of Dialogue on Disability, Biography, and Being Female in America* (Berkeley and Los Angeles: University of California Press, 2000); Rosemarie Garland-Thomson, "Feminist Disability Studies," *Signs: Journal of Women in Culture and Society* 30:2 (2005): 1557-87; Kay Gardiner Jamison, *An Unquiet Mind: A Memoir of Moods and Madness* (New York: Vintage, 1997); Harriet McBryde Johnson, *Too Late to Die Young: Nearly True Tales from a Life* (New York: Henry Holt, 2005); Simi Linton, *My Body Politic: A Memoir* (Ann Arbor: University of Michigan Press, 2005); and Audre Lorde, *The Cancer Journals: Special Edition* (San Francisco, Calif.: Aunt Lute Books, 2006).

See also: Nancy Mairs, *A Troubled Guest: Life and Death Stories* (Boston: Beacon, 2001), *Waist-High in the World: A Life among the Nondisabled* (Boston: Beacon, 1996), *Voice Lessons: On Becoming a (Woman) Writer* (Boston: Beacon, 1994), and *Plaintext: Deciphering a Woman's Life* (New York: Harper and Row, 1986); Mary Grimley Mason, *Working Against Odds: Stories of Disabled Women's Work Lives* (Boston: Northeastern University Press, 2004); Susannah B. Mintz, *Unruly Bodies: Life Writing by Women with Disabilities* (Chapel Hill: University of North Carolina Press, 2007); Lorna J. Moorhead, *Phone in the Fridge: Five Years with Multiple Sclerosis* (Orangevale, Calif.: Pathfinder Publishing, 2006) and *Coffee in the Cereal: The First Year with Multiple Sclerosis* (Oxnard, Calif.: Pathfinder Publishing, 2003); Peggy Munson, ed., *Stricken: Voices from the Hidden Epidemic of Chronic Fatigue Syndrome* (New York: Haworth Press, 2000); Lisa Roney, *Sweet Invisible Body: Reflections on a Life with Diabetes* (New York: Henry Holt, 1999); Marsha Saxton and Florence Howe, eds., *With Wings: An Anthology of Literature by and about Women with Disabilities* (New York: The Feminist Press, 1987); Shelley Tremain, ed., *Pushing the Limits: Disabled Dykes Produce Culture* (Ontario, Canada: Women's Press, 1996); Dorothy Wall, *Encounters With the Invisible: Unseen Illness, Controversy, and Chronic Fatigue Syndrome* (Dallas, Texas: Southern Methodist University Press, 2005); and Susan Wendell, *The Rejected Body: Feminist Philosophical Reflections on Disability* (New York: Routledge, 1996).

Recent insightful accounts by blind women, in particular, include: Sally Hobart Alexander, *Do You Remember the Color Blue? And Other Questions Kids Ask about Blindness* (New York: Viking, 2000) and *Taking Hold: My Journey Into Blindness* (New York: Macmillan, 1994); Beth Finke, *Long Time, No See* (Champaign: University of Illinois Press, 2003); Melissa J. Frame, *Blind Spots: The Communicative Performance of Visual Impairment in Relationships and Social Interaction* (Springfield, Ill.: Charles C. Thomas Publisher, 2004) and "What's Wrong With Her? The Stigmatizing Effects of an Invisible Stigma," *Disability Studies Quarterly* 20:3 (2000): 243-53; Georgina Kleege, *Blind Rage: Letters to Helen Keller* (Washington, D.C.: Guallaudet University Press, 2006) and *Sight Unseen* (New Haven: Yale University Press, 1999); Frances Lief Neer, *Dancing in the Dark* (San Francisco, Calif.: Wildstar Publishing, 1994); and Deborah Peifer, "Seeing is Be(liev)ing," in Victoria A. Brownworth and Susan Raffo, eds., *Restricted Access: Lesbians on Disability* (Seattle, Wash.: Seal Press, 1999): 31-34. Significant relevant narratives by blind men are: Stephen Kuusisto, *Eavesdropping: A Memoir of Blindness and Listening* (New York: Norton, 2006) and *Planet of the Blind: A Memoir* (New York: Dial, 1998); and Rod Michalko, *The Two-in-One: Walking with Smokie, Walking with Blindness* (Philadelphia: Temple University Press, 1998). See also: Madeline Milian and Jane N. Erin, eds., *Diversity and Visual Impairment: The Influence of Race, Gender, Religion, and Ethnicity on the Individual* (New York: American Foundation for the Blind Press, 2001).

Important collections, overviews, and personal narratives in the more general field of disability studies include: H-Dirksen L. Bauman, ed., *Open Your Eyes: Deaf Studies Talking* (Minneapolis: University of Minnesota Press, 2008); Douglas C. Baynton, *Forbidden Signs: American Culture and the Campaign against Sign Language* (Chicago: University of Chicago Press, 1996); James I. Charlton, *Nothing About Us Without Us: Disability Oppression and Empowerment* (Berkeley and Los Angeles: University of California Press, 2000); Mairian Corker and Tom Shakespeare, eds., *Disability/Postmodernity: Embodying Disability Theory* (London and New York: Continuum International Publishing Group, 2002); G. Thomas Couser, *Recovering Bodies: Illness, Disability, and Life Writing* (Madison: University of Wisconsin Press, 1997); Susan Crutchfield and Marcy Epstein, eds., *Points of Contact: Disability, Art, and Culture* (Ann Arbor: University of Michigan Press, 2000); Lennard J. Davis, *Bending Over Backwards: Essays on Disability and the Body* (New York: New York University Press, 2002) and *My Sense of Silence: Memoirs of a Childhood with Deafness* (Urbana: University of Illinois Press, 1999); Lennard J. Davis, ed., *The Disability Studies Reader, Second Edition* (New York: Routledge, 2006); Helen Deutsch and Felicity Nussbaum, eds. *"Defects": Engendering the Modern Body* (Ann Arbor: University of Michigan Press, 2000); Kenny Fries, *Body, Remember: A Memoir* (Madison: University of Wisconsin Press, 2003); Kenny Fries, ed., *Staring Back: The Disability Experience from the Inside Out* (New York: Plume, 1997); Rosemarie Garland-Thomson, *Extraordinary Bodies: Figuring Physical Disability in American Culture and Literature* (New York: Columbia University Press, 1997); and Kim Q. Hall, ed., "Special Issue: Feminist Disability Studies," *NWSA Journal* 14:8 (2002).

See also: Paul K. Longmore, *Why I Burned My Book: Essays on Disability* (Philadelphia: Temple University Press, 2003); Paul K. Longmore and Lauri Umansky, eds., *The New Disability History: American Perspectives* (New York: New York University Press,

2001); Robert McRuer, *Crip Theory: Cultural Signs of Queerness and Disability* (New York: New York University Press, 2006); Robert McRuer and Abby Wilkerson, eds., "Desiring Disability: Queer Theory Meets Disability Studies," *GLQ* 9:1-2 (2003); Rod Michalko, *The Difference that Disability Makes* (Philadelphia: Temple University Press, 2002); Diane Pothier and Richard Devlin, eds., *Critical Disability Theory: Essays in Philosophy, Politics, Policies, and Law* (Vancouver, Canada: University of British Columbia Press, 2006); Bonnie G. Smith and Beth Hutchison, eds., *Gendering Disability* (New Brunswick: Rutgers University Press: 2004); Sharon L. Snyder, Brenda Jo Brueggemann, and Rosemarie Garland-Thomson, eds., *Disability Studies: Enabling the Humanities* (New York: The Modern Language Association of America, 2002); Sharon L. Snyder and David T. Mitchell, *Cultural Locations of Disability* (Chicago: University of Chicago Press, 2006); and James C. Wilson and Cynthia Lewiecki-Wilson, eds., *Embodied Rhetorics: Disability in Language and Culture* (Carbondale: Southern Illinois University Press, 2001).

The southern New Mexico mountains are eloquently described in Robert Julyan and Carl Smith, *The Mountains of New Mexico* (Albuquerque: University of New Mexico Press, 2006); and represented in photographs in Peter Greene, *Mike Butterfield's Guide to the Mountains of New Mexico* (Santa Fe: New Mexico Magazine Press, 2006). For further geological and wilderness information on the remote areas described in *Traveling Blind*, see: Russel E. Clemons, Paige W. Christianson, and Hal L. James, *Southwestern New Mexico: Scenic Trips to the Geologic Past No. 10* (Socorro: New Mexico Bureau of Mines and Mineral Resources, 1980, reprinted 2000); and Bob Julyan and Tom Till, *New Mexico Wilderness Areas: The Complete Guide* (Boulder, Colo.: Westcliffe Publishers, 1998).

A rare historical study of Hachita is George Hilliard, *Adios Hachita: Stories of a New Mexico Town* (Silver City, N.M.: High Lonesome Books, 1998); further background appears in: Linda

G. Harris and Pamela Porter, *Ghost Towns Alive: Trips to New Mexico's Past* (Albuquerque: University of New Mexico Press, 2003); and William Least Heat Moon, *Blue Highways: A Journey Into America* (Boston: Atlantic Monthly Press, Little, Brown and Company, 1982): 155-60. Music celebrating the spirit of the Bootheel referred to in Chapter 1 is available on the audio CD by Kip Calahan, "Cowboys, Cowgirls, Round-ups, and Rodeos," (Rodeo, N.M.: Kip Calahan, 2003). The classic western novel set in the Big Hatchet region is Louis L'Amour, *Shalako* (New York: Bantam, 1962). Notable recent writings by women conveying desert sensibilities can be found in Susan Wittig Albert et al, eds., *What Wildness Is This: Women Write about the Southwest* (Austin: University of Texas Press, 2007).